Military English for officers

군간부를 위한
군사영어

박경배 · 김지한 共著

 21세기사

Two years have already passed since COVID-19 began. Education and life at colleges caused by the virus have also changed a lot situation from the past. Some say that history may be divided into pre COVID-19 and post COVID-19 civilizations, so it seems that it's now a world to live with COVID-19.

More than 30 years after I was discharged from military, writing defence english for Non commissioned officers felt quite unfamiliar with military training and terms. Still, as I have military experience, I soon became familiar with military defence terms, but I think many misinterpretation in many area. Nevertheless, I comfort myself that there will be some wrong contents, because I wrote it as simply as possible simple about military.

This book is about NCO and consist of a total of 9 chapters. For learners who hate English extremely, games related to disassembly and assembly of firearms were included in many parts. I think it will be effective learning by encountering English while playing games.

Chap 1 and 2 contain simple contents related to NCO and the Army.

Chap 3 explains the types of rifle and the principle of firing.

Chap 4 and 5 briefly describe the education and training that soldiers should receive in the Korean Army, and explain the abbreviations of military terms used in the military.

In order to become a noncommissioned officer, you must take a military officer writing test. For this, Chap 6 to 9 explained basic computational ability, basic statistical ability, basic chart understanding ability, and basic chart writing ability for mathematical ability.

When I started writing this books, I tried to give up because I felt like I was wasting my time, but I was able to complete it with the help of my 1st son who will join KATUSA soon and my 2nd son who became a student at SKK Univ. this year, Thanks for them. Finally, I would like to express my gratitude to Prof. Kim Ji-han, the head of the Department of Defense Equipment, for his great help in writing the book.

God bless everyone ...
On the eve of the new year, 2022.
대표 저자 박경배

Covid-19가 시작된지 벌써 2년이 지나가고 있다. 코로나 바이러스에 의한 대학의 교육과 생활도 양상이 예전과 많이 달라졌다. 누군가는 역사가 코로나 이전의 문명과 코로나 이후의 문명으로 나뉠 수도 있다고 할 만큼 이제는 코로나와 더불어 살아나가야 할 세상이 된 것 같다. 군대를 제대한지 벌써 30년이 넘어가는 이 시점에 부사관을 위한 국방영어를 집필하면서 군대의 훈련이나 군대의 용어가 사뭇 낯설게 느껴졌지만 그래도 군 경험이 있다 보니 곧 국방 용어에 친숙해지기는 했으나 많은 부분에서 오역이 있을 것이라 생각 된다. 그럼에도 불구하고 가능하면 간단하게 군대와 관련된 내용으로 집필했으니 큰 무리가 없을 거라고 스스로 위안을 삼는다.

이 책은 부사관과 관련된 내용으로 9장으로 구성 되었다. 영어만 접하면 머리 아픈 학습자를 위하여 많은 부분에서 총기의 분해와 조립과 관련된 게임을 포함하였다. 게임을 하면서 영어를 접하며 효과적인 학습이 되리라 생각한다.

1장과 2장에서는 부사관과 육군에 관련된 간단한 내용이 포함되어 있다.
3장에서는 소총의 종류에 대해 설명하였으며 총기의 발사 원리를 설명하였다.
4장과 5장에서는 대한민국 육군에서 병사가 받아야할 교육과 훈련을 간단히 기술하였으며 군에서 사용되는 군사 용어의 약자를 설명하였다.
부사관이 되기 위해서는 군 간부필기 시험을 보아야 한다. 이를 위해 6장에서 9장까지는 자료해석과 관련된 내용으로 수리능력에 대해 기초연산능력, 기초통계능력, 기초도표이해능력 그리고 기초 도표 작성능력에 대해 설명하였다. 영어를 배우며 부사관 시험에 꼭 필요한 내용을 학습도록 하였다.

교재 집필을 시작하면서 진도는 나가지 않고 시간만 낭비하는 것 같아 포기하려고도 하였으나 곧 카튜사에 입대하는 큰아들의 도움과 올해 성균관 유생이 된 둘째 아들의 도움으로 완성할 수 있었기에 아들들에게 지면을 빌려 고마움을 표한다. 끝으로 책의 집필에 큰 도움을 주신 국방장비과 학과장 김지한 교수님께 감사의 말씀을 드립니다.

2022년 새해가 시작되기 바로전날
대표 저자 박경배

PART I   Military English for officers

PART II Data Interpretation

Chapter 9 **Analysis and Making Ability of Chart   / 149**

APPENDIX

PART Ⅰ

Military English for officers

Chapter 1

NCO and Military Rank

1 Non Commissioned Officer Academy and Rank

1.1 Non Commissioned Officer

(Ref:https://goarmy.mil.kr:447/goarmy/2717/subview.do)

Non Commissioned Officers who plays a pivotal role in military

NCO pursue honor by shining on his own and become proud. They should be able to act

vocabulary

> **pivotal:** a. 중추적인　**pursue:** v. 추구하다, 추적하다
> **proud:** a. 자랑스러워하는, 자랑스러운 (→house-proud)　**aware of:** a. 알고 있는
> **principles:** n. 원칙　**constructive:** a 건설적인 n. constructiveness
> **maintain:** n. 유지
> **suggestion:** n.제안, 의견　**judgement:** n. 의견　**staff sergeant:** n. 하사
> **community:** n. 공동체　**contribute:** v. 기여하다　**appointment:** n 임명, 직위
> **Guaranteed:** a. 보장된　**state official:** n 국가 공무원　**dormitory:** n. 기숙사
> **lifelong job:** n.평생직장　**compare A to B:** v. A와 B를 비교하다
> **accommodation:** n. 숙소, 합의　**expenditure:** n. 지출, 소비　**service:** n. 복무
> **provision:** n. 예비, 준비, 설비　**accommodation:** n. 시설　**loan:** n. 대출, 대여
> **pension:** n. 연금　**specialized:** a. 전문의, 분화한　**combat:** n. 전투
> **warrant:** n. 근거, 보장　**tuition:** n. 수업　**operate:** v. 작동되다, 가동되다

aware of the principles that they have to keep as social humans. They should be able to make constructive suggestions with correct thinking and judgement in everything, maintaining a sense of community that know how to care for others rather than individuals. They are talented people who have the expertise to contribute to their troops and military.

Guaranteed a stable job as a state official

If you pass a prescribed examination(written and personality tests, physical examinations, physical fitness tests, interview evaluations), you will receive a noncommissioned officer's appointment training. After that training they were appointed as a staff sergeant. If they become a staff sergeant, their status is elevated as a state official and selected by supporting long-term service, they will be guaranteed a stable lifelong job.

Get a large sum of money in the shortest time

Compared to the member of the general society with similar educational backgrounds, the military provides accommodation and meal, so there is no need for expenditure on clothing etc. Up to 50 million won can be saved if 60% of the salary is saved between non commissioned officer's four-year service.

With various welfare benefits, the real wage is higher

With the provision of single accommodation, official residence, military apartment, supply of special apartments by the Military Mutual Aid Association, and loan benefits of low interest they can achieve their dream of buying their own house early.

Served for more than 20 years and guarantees his retirement through pension benefits.

If you are discharging from the military after serving for more than 20 years, you will be given pension benefits(succession to 70% spouse when yo die) and various benefits such as the saddle of the National Cemetery.

After serving for more than 33 years, you will be treated as a person of national merit for the benefit of the Order of Patriots and Veterans Affairs.

Working in a specialized field where individual majors and abilities can be exercised

Depending on an individual's major and qualification, you can perform specialized tasks in various fields such as combat, technology, and administration. if you meet certain qualification requirements, opportunities to advance to warrant officers are given.

Providing opportunities of self-development

Opportunities for self-development, such as college, cyber college, university, and graduate school, will be given. In addition you will be get opportunity to obtain a certificate by taking the National Technical Qualification Test (twice a year) hosted by the Army.

Support for a wide range of children's education

Children of long-term service NCO shall be paid the full tuition for middle and high school students. If they go to college, scholarships will be paid and tuition loan will be provided by the state at full interest.

Education conditions are guaranteed by providing military-operated dormitories to children studying in large cities.

1.2 History of NCO and Honorary Ceremony

(Ref : https://nco.mil.kr:456/nco/2313/subview.do)

History

Period	Year	Event
1895~1949	1895 (Emperor Kojong 32 Y.)	The non commissioned officer system is started, 3 ranks(Chamgyo-Boogyo-Junggyo)
	1945.02	The Liberation Army, 4 ranks(3 ranks +Special Officer)
	1946.01	National Defence Guard, 6 ranks (Chamgyo-Boogyo-TeukmooBoogyo-Junggyo-Teukmoojunggyo-Dea TMJgyo)
	1946.12	6 ranks (sergeant) (staff - second - first - second master - first master - major)
	1949.01	4 ranks(sergeant) (staff-first-master-major), Mandatory service(3 years)
1962~1989	1962.04	3 ranks (staff-first-master), Mandatory service(4 years), Retirement age(45 years)
	1967.02	Confirmed of the chief executive officer system and Operation.
	1980.12	Mandatory service (long-term 7 years, short-term 4 years), Retirement age (50 years)
	1989.03	4 ranks (staff-first-master-1st master), Retirement age (53 years)

vocabulary

liberation: n. 해방, 석방   **sergeant:** n. 병장   **mandatory:** a. 법에 정해진, 의무적인
insignia: n. 휘장(배지)   **courtesy:** n. 공손함, 정중함
National Defence Guard: 국가 방위군   **Mandatory service:** 의무 복무,
Retirement age: 은퇴연령   **confirm:** n. 확인
chief executive officer system: 주임상사 제도
attachment position: 부착 위치   **corp:** n. 군단   **inherit:** v. 상속하다   **dedicate:** v. 바치다
praise: v. 기도하다   **cultivate:** v. 수련하다, 연마하다   **classify:** v. 분류하다   **mainstay:** n. 중심
expertise: n. 전문성   **authority:** n. 권위   **adversity:** n. 역경, 불행

Period	Year	Event
1994~1996	1994.01	4 ranks (staff-first-master-major), Retirement age (55 years)
	1995.06	Changing the name of the position (Appointed Ser.→Administrative officer/ Business officer/ Subcommittee Leader)
	1996.10	Improvement of insignia type and attachment position.
2001~ Present	2001.03	Name Improvement(Sergeant → NCO)
	2005.01	Decide and operate the courtesy of Command sergeant major(CSM)

Honor Ceremony

① Entrance Ceremony

Congratulations on entering the non commissioned officer academy, A ceremony will be held at related education corps on the night of entrance day in order to motivate and resolve the executive curriculum to be run for 13~18 weeks,

② Successive Ceremony of a human bullet 10 warrior.

As a non commissioned officer trainee who wants to serve as a model for the duty of a soldier dedicated to the country, a ceremony is held in front of the human bullet 10 warrior bronze statue to inherit the spirit of sacrifice, loyalty, and strong military spirit of the human bullet 10 warrior who were heroically killed at the pigeon highlands of Song-ak Mountain.

③ Birth Ceremony

Birth ceremony will be held for praise the hard work during the training period to become a non commissioned officer and promote motivation among their candidates and cultivate the confidence about field unit's mission.

1.3　Rank

(Ref:https://www.army.mil.kr/webapp/user/indexSub.do?codyMenuSeq=219387&siteId=english)

The status of military classified into Field grade officer, Company grade officer, Non Commissioned officer and Enlisted(soldier) for mission purpose.

Field grade Officer

"Officers are mainstay in the military. Therefore, the officers are aware of the importance of the responsibility and acquire the expertise and skills necessary for performing own duties, build up healthy character and work hard to train mind and body, and should have insight and authority to take proper judgment and action even in adversity with respect and trust from subordinates by fairly treating them, complying with laws, and taking the initiative." (In Officer's Duty)

Officer is divided a field officer and a General.
Generals are the highest rank in the military and their status is represented by star insignia.
Brigadier General is the lowest rank among Generals in the military and represented by one star insignia. The next higher rank is Major General by two star. Lieutenant General is represented by three star insignia and is rank just below General that has a four star.

---

vocabulary

Field grade officer: 영관장교　**Company grade officer:** 위관장교
work hart to: ~을 위해 노력하다　**adversity with:** 역경 속에서도
subordinate: a. 아래의, Brigadier　**General:** 준장　**Major General:** 소장,
Lieutenant General: 중장, General: 대장
lieutenant colonel: n. 중령　**colonel:** n. 대령
bamboo: n. 대나무　**greenness:** n. 초록색　**rhombus:** n. 마름모　**will:** n. 의지
form: a. 모양, 형상 **examination:** n. 시험　**lieutenant:** n. 중위(first~), 소위(second~)
initiative: n, 발의　**compliance:** n. 승낙, 추종　**internal:** a. 내부의, 안의 n. 본질
enlisted soldier: n. 사병　**pride:** n. 자랑, 자존심, 긍지
underneath: a. ~아래의, ~지배하의　**gather:** v. 모으다.
mobilize: v. 동원하다, 전시체제로 바꾸다.
indispensable: a. 불가결의, 없어서는 안 될　**maintenance:** n. 유지, 지속

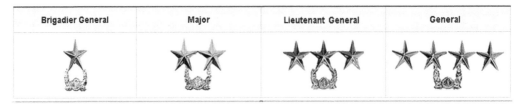

Brigadier General	Major	Lieutenant General	General

The ranks of field officers are divided into Major, Lieutenant Colonel and Colonel. Their "*insignia symbolized bamboo and classified according to the number of bamboo.*"
(Ref:https://www.army.mil.kr/webapp/user/indexSub.do?codyMenuSeq=219387&siteId=english)

Major is represented one bamboo insignia and Lieutenant Colonel is two and Colonel is three. Bamboo symbolizes the ever greenness of four seasons, strong spirit, and fidelity.

Major	Lieutenant Colonel	Colonel

Company grade Officer

Company grade Officer refer to all beginner officers. They are higher than non commissioned officers and lower than field officers. "*Company officer's rhombus symbolizes the beginning officers strong will of the protection of the nation and is expressed in a form of strong and unbreakable diamond.*"
(Ref:https://www.army.mil.kr/webapp/user/indexSub.do?codyMenuSeq=219387&siteId=english)

warrant officer	2nd Lieutenant	1st Lieutenant	Captain

The lowest rank among company grade officer is a warrant officer who is treated equally as an officer. In order to become a warrant officer, it is necessary to pass the promotion examination of a warrant officer above Master sergeant among non commissioned officers. A warrant officer's insignia is one yellow rhombus.

Just above the rank of warrant officer is second Lieutenant whose insignia is one silver diamond. First Lieutenant's insignia is two silver diamonds and Captain is represented own status by three diamonds.

Non Commissioned Officer

"NCO is an executive who maintains the unit's tradition and protects it's honor. Therefore they should be familiar with their duties, take the initiative and setting examples in everything, supervise compliance with law and order, and guide education, training, internal affairs life of the Enlisted. In addition to, they should identify and lead Enlists, prevent safety accidents, and strive to manage various equipment and supplies."
(In NCO's Duty)

In 1996, Non-commissioned officers' insignia was revised from the past insignia on which their insignia was marked on top of that of the enlisted soldiers causing it to look too big. So to arouse their pride and to make it look like the insignia of the officers, they added the Mugunghwa sign underneath their insignia.
(Ref:https://www.army.mil.kr/webapp/user/indexSub.do?codyMenuSeq=219387&siteId=english)

Staff Sergeant	Sergeant First Class	Master Sergeant	Sergeant Major

* (Ref:ROKA)

Enlisted

Enlisted refer to a soldier of the lowest status constituting the military. They don't even have precious status and special knowledge of a field officer also long career and expertise by non commissioned officer.

Therefore, in principle, Enlisted form a unit with several soldier gathered under one or more NCO and a officers. They are members of the lowest rank in the military, but at the same time they are also the rank that can mobilize the largest number. Infantry and gunner etc are the majority of combat power in a branch of military service where is important the number of troops. They are also indispensible members in simple tasks such as armour, air force, navy maintenance.

(Ref:https://namu.wiki/w/병(군인))

Enlisted's insignia is as follow(Ref:ROKA)

Rank	Insignia	Note
Private		Private is the lowest lank in the military.
Private First Class		After three to four months from the Private, become Private First Class.
Corporal/ Specialist		*In 1962, enlisted ranks were divided into four, and those who were in upper rank of the enlisted were called corporal.*
Sergent		*The term sergeant was used to signify the head of enlisted ranks.*

1.4 Installing a weapon game

Let's find out the types of weapons which soldier can own and broaden our understanding of firearms through the disassembly and assembly of weapons. To this end, it is necessary to install a game for disassembling and assembling of weapons driven by smart phone.

Let's install the game in following steps.

step 1 Execute "Play Store" App. on wallpaper of smart phone.

step 2 Write "weapon field stripping" in search window and install the game to press "play" button .

step 3 Complete the installation, you can see the following icon on the wallpaper.

Game explanation

The screen of game consist of five parts as shown in the image below.

Part 1 : If you click the button, related information is displayed in Part 2 as below.

① Result of game 게임결과   ② Achievement 성취도   ③ Weapon Information 무기정보
④ Setup 설정   ⑤ SNS

Part 2 : Display about 5 information of Part 1.

Part 3 : If you select weapon in Part 5, related weapon is displayed.

Part 4 : Select one out of the following three games.

① Instruction : As button related to the disassembly and assembly of weapons, three modes are displayed as follows.

Video tutorial : Mode of linking related weapons to YouTube.

Disassembly : Mode to train the disassembly process for the weapons involved.

Assembly : Mode to train the assembly process for the weapons related.

② Time tutorial : As the button related to the disassembly and assembly time of weapons, three mode are displayed as follows

Disassembly : Mode to measure the disassembly time of related weapons.

Assembly : Mode to measure the assembly time of related weapons.

Disassembly/Assembly : A Mode that measures time to assembly after disassembling related weapons.

③ Free mode : You can see the internal structure of the weapons and the principle of bullets firing and control the speed of bullets firing. Therefore, there are two modes that allow you to control the speed at which bullets are fired and see the internal structure.

Control the speed of bullet firing.

Making the inside of the weapons transparent.

Show the other side of the weapon.

Part 5 : You can select various weapons. If you chose one weapon, related weapons display as shown right side. Currently weapons serviced are Revolver, Pistol, Shotgun, Sniper Rifle, Submachine Gun(SMG), Assault Rifle, Automatic Machine Gun and Anti-tank Rifle.

We will learn about disassembly and assembly of some of the aforementioned weapons next chapters.

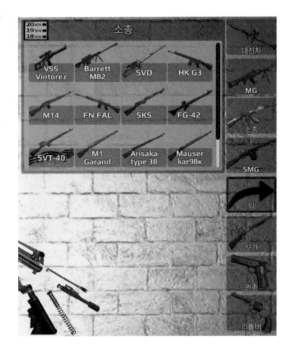

1.Q Question

1. What do you think are the advantages of NCO?

2. Which of the four attributes in the following examples is the wrong classification?

   ① Master Sergeant   ② Captain
   ③ Sergeant First Class   ④ Sergeant Major

3. What is the goal of a non-commissioned officer?

4. Translate the following sentence into Korean.

   4-1. The Republic of Korea Army is the center of national defence.

   4-2. The purpose of the military's existence is to ultimately win the war and preserve the state.

   4-3. ROKA contributes to curbing war from breaking out.

   4-4. Guarantee of simultaneous consolidation for management of combat power by networked command control.

   4-5. A non-commissioned officers are fluent with their duties, take the initiative in everything, and supervise soldiers' compliance with laws and orders.

5. Translate the following sentence into English.

5-1. 부사관은 군대에서 장교와 병사 사이에 교량적 역할을 수행한다.

5-2. 부사관은 군대 내에서 장비운용, 무기의 정비 그리고 부대 관리 등의 전문가로 임무수행을 한다.

5-3. 대한민국의 안녕과 미래는 대한민국 국군들에게 달려 있다.

1 N Note

1.R Reference

https://goarmy.mil.kr:447/goarmy/2717/subview.do

https://www.army.mil.kr/webapp/user/indexSub.do?codyMenuSeq=213458&siteId=army

https://www.nco.mil.kr:456/nco/2283/subview.do

https://nco.mil.kr:456/nco/2313/subview.do

https://www.goarmy.mil.kr:447/goarmy/2667/subview.do

https://www.goarmy.mil.kr:447/sites/goarmy/images/sub/2020_bintro.pdf

https://namu.wiki/w/병(군인)

https://play.google.com/store/apps/details?id=com.segasvd.WeaponFieldStrip

facebook.com/sega.svd

http://www.youtube.com/c/SegaSvd

Chapter 2

Introduce of ROKA

2 Introduce ROKA(Republic OF Korea Army)

(REF:https://www.army.mil.kr/webapp/user/indexSub.do?codyMenuSeq=213410&siteId=army)

(REF:https://www.army.mil.kr/webapp/user/indexSub.do?codyMenuSeq=215633&siteId=army)

2.1 Object of ROKA

Main Objects of ROKA as the main force of national defence.

vocabulary

contribute to: ~ 기여하다, 공헌하다   deterrence: n, 단념시킴, 제지, 방해물

break out: v. 발발하다   ordinarily: adv. 통상시에, 보통   sacrifice: n. 희생 제물

preparedness: n, 준비, 전시에 대한 군비   military preparedness: 군비 태세

democratic: a. 민주주의의,   according to: ~에 따라

implement: v. 도구를 주다   tangible: a. 실체적인, 확실한

advancement: n. 전진, 진출, 진보   strategic: a. 전략상의, 전략상 중요한

desperate: a. 무모한, 필사적인   assure: v. 보증하다, 보장하다

diplomacy: n. 외교, 외교술,   in charge of: ~ 의 책임 있는

tangible or intangible: 유 무형의   foster: v. 육성하다

Assurer: n. 보장자   strategic deterrence: 전략적 억제

social competitiveness: 사회적 경쟁력   executive: n. 지도자, 임원, 간부

① Contribute to war deterrence

The purpose of ROKA's existence is to ultimately win the war and preserve nation, but it's best to win without fighting. To this end, it means that our ROKA should be contribute to preventing war from breaking out by establishing ordinarily a through military preparedness.

② Achieve victory in all ground battles

When the war broke out due to failure to war deterrence, it means that our ROKA contributes to the end of the war by achieve victory in all ground battles in a short period of time at the minimum sacrifice according to the given mission.

③ Serve people's interests

It means that ROKA is the army of the people in charge of democratic citizenship education for soldiers, taking the lead in implementing national policies and active supporting the safety and convenience of people.

④ Build the strong and elite force

It means that preparation for various security threats and high-tech information and scientific warfare expected in the future, ROKA must maintain tangible or intangible combat force at all times by propelling constant elitism and advancement in the spirits Yu-bi-mu-hwan.

Three roles of ROKA

① Assurer

- strategic deterrence
- operational quick response
- desperate resistance defence, assure safety

② Builder

- Trust formation of South between North and support for peace building
- Support safety of people
- Maintaining international peace and military diplomacy

③ **Connector**

- Enhance the value of mandatory service
- Fostering executives with social competitiveness
- Contributing to science and technology, industry and economic development

2.2 Organization of ROKA

(ref:https://www.army.mil.kr/webapp/user/indexSub.do?codyMenuSeq=213411&siteId=army)

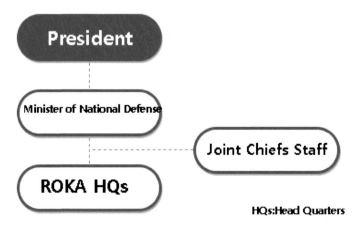

* Organization of ROKA (Ref : Organization of ROKA)

- **President:** The supreme commander in charge of the ROKA.

- **Minister of National Defense**: Receives orders from president and commands and supervises Chairman of the Joint Chiefs of Staff and Chief of Staff ROKA.

- **Chairman of the Joint Chiefs of Staff:** Receives orders from the Minister of National Defense and commands and supervises Operational Force of each service whose main duties are fighting battles.

- **Chief of Staff ROKA:** Command and supervise the ROKA by the order of the Minister of National Defense, except for the command and supervision of each military operational force whose main mission is combat.

Subordinate of ROKA

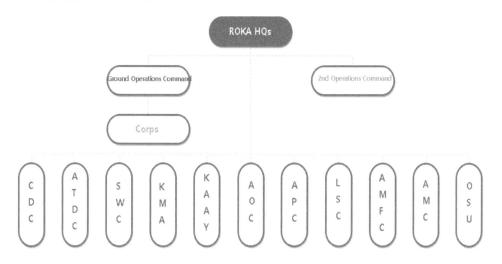

Subordinate of ROKA

- CDC: Capital Defense Command 수도방위 사령부
- ATDC: Army Training & Doctrine command 육군교육사령부
- SWC: Special Warfare Command 특전사령부
- KMA: Korea Military Academy 육군사관학교
- KAAY: Korea Army Academy at Yeoungcheon 육군 3사관학교
- AAC: Army Aviation Command 항공작전 사령부
- APC: Army Personnel Command 인사사령부
- LSC: Logistics Support Command 군수사령부
- AMFC: Army Mobilization Force Command 동원사령부
- AMC: Army Missile Command 미사일사령부
- OSU: Other Service Units 기타 부대

The ROKA HQs is organized Ground Operations Command, 2nd Operations Command, CDC, ATEC, SWC, KMA, KAAY, AOC, APC, LSC, AMFC, AMC and OSU.

The Ground Operations Command is in charge of the front line, 2nd Operations Commnand is in charge of the back area and Capital Defence Command is in charge of the Seoul area. The other units carry out special warfare, aviation operation, supporting continue strategy, education and training, reserve force elitism, administrative support.

2.3 Press release related to the NCO

(ref: Press release of Korea Combat Training Center. 2021.9.9)

From September 9th, the Korea Army organized a battalion led by 450 beginner Non Commissioned Officers at Korea Combat Training Center(KCTC) in In-Je, Kwangwon-do, KCTC training began on the 4th, day and night in a row with professional opposing forces units.

This is first time that the Army has organized a combat team which is composed of beginner Non Commissioned Officers to train for KCTC.

The training is designed to help beginner NCOs, who will be the backbone of military combat capabilities and lead the Army's combat capabilities, master combat skills through actual combat experience and cultivate combat leaderships as platoon combat commanders.

There are about 450 trainees currently training in the "NCOs Beginner Leader Course" at each military school(NCO, Artillery, Engineering, and Chemical, Biological, Radiological) and to support this, more than 80 troops will participate in the training, a total of 530 soldiers will train with KCTC specialized opposing force units under the battalion combat team of beginner NCOs.

The new NCOs are mainly compose of combatants under the company level, they conduct combat training in the phase of attack and defense operations for two days at a time and for

vocabulary

battalion: n. 대대 **day and night in a row:** 밤낮으로
composed of: ~로 구성된 **backbone:** 척추, 근본, 중추
cultivate combat: 전투를 전개하다. 경작하다. 재배하다.(cultivate)
trainee: n. 훈련병 **Artillery:** n. 포병 **Engineering:** n. 공병, 기술자
participate in: ~ 참가하다 **the phase of:** ~ 국면
tactical: a. 전술적인 **manless:** n. 무인 **high-intensity:** 고강도
quarantine: n. 격리 **intensive:** a. 집중적인

four days without sleep.

The "MILES Drone System" which embodies tactical movements to hit enemy with attack drones and defends it as a scientific training system was also used for training. So NCOs experienced the future battlefield and manless combat system.

The safety measure of combatants have also been thoroughly prepared. In order to block COVID-19, high-intensity quarantine rules at the level of 4 stages of distancing are applied even before training, As a measure to prevent accidents, about 30 safety guard are operated throughout the training ground to conduct training with an emergency patient evacuation and treatment system in place.

Meanwhile, The Army is continuing practical and intensive tactical training using science combat training, including "KCTC Training for new officers", from "KCTC training between training units" and "KCTC training for new non commissioned officers," where two brigade-level units engage with each other for the first time this year.

2.4 The part name of the Firearms

2.4.1 Revolver Specifications

A handgun refers to a personal firearm that can be handled with one or both hands. A revolver is put bullets in a cylinder instead of a magazine, and whenever it is fired, the cylinder rotates to fire a bullet. You can be seen a lot the weapon in western American movie.

It is durable, reliable, and mostly uses strong bullets. However, most of these are six or seven consecutive rounds, so the number of bullets is not enough, takes some time to reload, and the recoil is severe.

* Revolvoer

The part name

① catch cylinder : Pull backwards.

② ammo cartridge : Supply 6~7 bullets.

③ remover ammo : Pull forward.

④ grip screw : Screw for disassembly and assembly.

⑤ grip : The part where you hold it with your hands.

⑥ cylinder assembly pins : Pull out pins.

⑦ side plate : Cover of notch.

⑦-1,2 : Side plate screw.

⑧ notch : Notch rear.

⑨ barrel : The path which bullets go out.

Revolver Spec.

Data	Specifications
Type	Revolver
Manufacturer	Colt's Patent Firearms Manufacturing Co.
Used by	United States, United Kingdom, Canada
Used Wars	World war I, II, Korea War, Vietnam War
Weight/Length	1.1Kg / 273mm
Barrel length	140mm
Action	Double-Action
Feed system	6-round cylinder
Sights	fixed blade front, notch rear

2.4.2 The process of disassembling revolver

step 1 Open the cylinder(cartridge) and Pull ① back to open the cylinder.

step 2 Pull ③ back to remove the ammo cartridges.

step 3 Turn the screw ④ to remove the grip plates.

4-1 : Place the cylinder back to its initial state.

4-2 : Pull out the cylinder assembly pins ⑥.

4-3 : Remove the cylinder(ammo cartridges).

Turn the screw 7-1,2 to remove slide the plate.

Complete disassembly.

2.4.3 Assembly process

The process of assembly is the inverse process of disassembly.

step 1 Attach the side plate⑦

step 2 Attach the cylinder assembly②

step 3 Attach the grip⑤

Your best records (sec)

Disassembly	Assembly	Disassembly & Assembly

2.Q   Question

1. What are the three roles of ROKA?

2. Which of the following is not the ROKA' three major goals?

　① Warfare deterrence　　　　　　　② Build Elite
　③ Attack Enemy　　　　　　　　　　④ Serve people

3. What is the duty of Chief of ROKA?

4. Translate the following sentence into Korean.

　4-1. The other units carry out special warfare, aviation operation, supporting continue strategy, education and training, reserve force elitism, administrative support.

　4-2. A handgun refers to a personal fire extinguisher that can be handled with on or both hands.

　4-3. The purpose of ROKA's existence is to ultimately win the war and preserve nation, but it's best to win without fighting.

　4-4. The safety measure of combatants have also been thoroughly prepared.

　4-5. This is first time that the Army has organized a combat team composed of beginner Non Commissioned Officers to train for KCTC.

5. Translate the following sentence into English.

5-1. 대한민국 육군은 국가 방위의 중심군으로서 전쟁 억제에 기여한다.

5-2. 육군 참모총장은 대통령의 명령에 따라 육군을 지휘하고 감독한다.

5-3. 군의 존재 목적은 전쟁에서 승리하여 국가를 보존하는 일이다.

2.N Note

2.R Reference

https://goarmy.mil.kr:447/goarmy/2717/subview.do

https://www.army.mil.kr/webapp/user/indexSub.do?codyMenuSeq=213410&siteId=army

https://www.army.mil.kr/webapp/user/indexSub.do?codyMenuSeq=215633&siteId=army

https://nco.mil.kr:456/nco/2313/subview.do

https://www.goarmy.mil.kr:447/goarmy/2667/subview.do

https://ko.wikipedia.org/wiki/대한민국_육군의_부대

facebook.com/sega.svd

http://www.youtube.com/c/SegaSvd

Chapter 3

Sorts of Rifle

3 Sorts of Rifle

(Ref: https://ko.wikipedia.org/wiki/자동소총)

(Ref: https://ia800502.us.archive.org/35/items/FM23-92006/FM23-92006.pdf)

(Ref: https://www.logsa.army.mil/etms/data/A/026397.pdf)

An automatic rifle is a firearm that is automatically reloaded after a bullet is fired, and refers to a rifle capable of semi-automatic shooting or fully automatic shooting. Rifles that manually reload one foot at a time include bolt action, pump action, and lever action methods.

vocabulary

rear: a. 뒤쪽
include: v. 포함하다   **procedure:** n. 순서, 수순   **eject:** v. 몰아내다
cock: v. 공이치기를 당기다   **bayonet:** n. 총검

3.1 The name of each part - M16

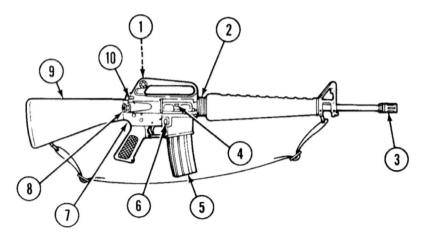

Each part name of M16

① rear sight 가늠쇠

② hand guard slip ring / delta ring   총열 덮개 고정 링/델타 링

③ flash suppressor 소염기

④ ejection port cover 탄피 배출 덮개

⑤ cartridge magazine 탄창

⑥ magazine catch button 탄창 멈칫

⑦ lower receiver 아래 몸통

⑧ forward assist   노리쇠 전진기

⑨ shoulder gun stock 개머리 판

⑩ charging/clocking handle 장전 손잡이

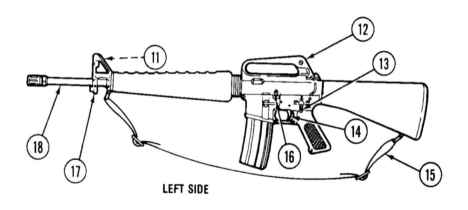

LEFT SIDE

The other side

⑪ front sight 가늠쇠

⑫ carrying handle 운반손잡이

⑬ selector lever 조정간

⑭ 방아쇠 trigger　⑮ small arms sling 멜빵

⑯ bolt catch 노리쇠 앞부분

⑰ bayonet stud 칼꽂이　⑱ front barrel 총열 앞부분

M16A2 Field-stripped

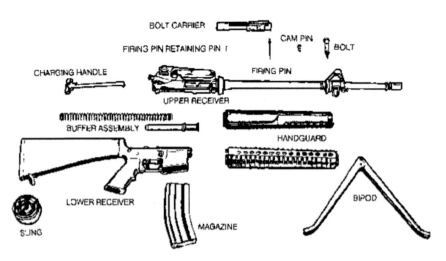

3.2 The procedure of shooting bullets

M16 bolt assembly M16 노리쇠 뭉치

The breechblock (bolt) is a component that closes the back of the chamber in case of an explosion in the firearm. Usually in Korean, the term Norisoe refers to a bolt that operates mechanically connected to a bolt carrier, which is used for rifles.

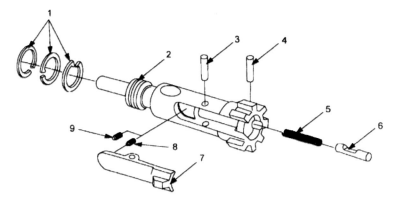

The part name of M16 bolt assembly

1 RING, BOLT

2 BOLT

3 PIN, EXTRACTOR

4 PIN, SPRING EJECTOR

5 SPRING, HELICAL, COMPRESSION EJECTOR

6 EJECTOR, CARTRIDGE

7 EXTRACTOR, CARTRIDGE

8 SPRING ASSEMBLY, EXT EXTRACTOR (M16A2)

9 SPRING ASSEMBLY, EXT EXTRACTOR (M4 ND M4A1)(BLACK)

---

vocabulary

breechblock: n. 노리쇠   **chamber:** n. 탄약실   **explosion:** n. 폭발
extractor: n. 추출기   **ejector:** n. 배출기
engage: ~관여하다. 결합되다
charging: 장전   **thrust:** v. 밀치다. 찌르다   **claw:** n. 발톱, 집게발
rim: a. 테두리, 가장자리   **lug:** n. 돌출부, v. 나르다, 끌다
exert: v. 가하다, 노력하다

Procedure

Feeding → Loading → Locking → Firing → Unlocking → Extracting → Ejecting → Cocking

① Feeding 송탄

As the bolt carrier group moves rearward, it engages the buffer assembly and compresses the action spring into the lower receiver extension. When the bolt carrier group clears the top of the magazine, the expansion of the magazine spring forces the follower and a new round up into the path of the forward movement of the bolt. The expansion of the action spring sends the buffer assembly and bolt carrier group forward with enough force to strip a new round from the magazine.

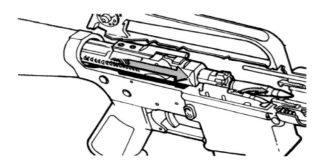

② loading, charging 장전

As the bolt carrier group continues to move forward, the face of the bolt thrusts the new round into the chamber. At the same time, the extractor claw grips the rim of the cartridge, and the ejector is compressed

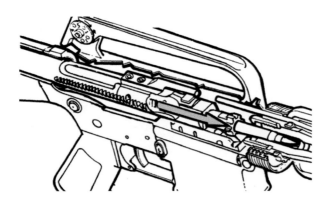

③ bolt locking 노리쇠 잠김

As the bolt carrier group moves forward, the bolt is kept in its most forward position by the bolt cam pin riding in the guide channel in the upper receiver. Just before the bolt locking lugs make contact with the barrel extension, the bolt cam pin emerges from the guide channel. The pressure exerted by the contact of the bolt locking lugs and barrel extension causes the bolt cam pin to move along the cam track (located in the bolt carrier) in a counterclockwise direction, rotating the bolt locking lugs in line behind the barrel extension locking lugs. The rifle is then ready to fire.

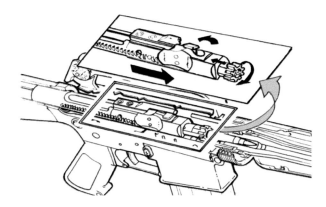

④ firing 발사

With a round in the chamber, the hammer cocked, and the selector on SEMI, the firer squeezes the trigger. The trigger rotates on the trigger pin, depressing the nose of the trigger and disengaging the notch on the bottom on the hammer.

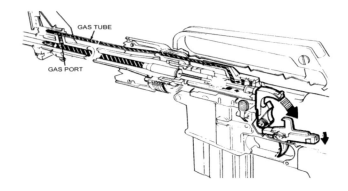

⑤ **unlocking bolt 노리쇠 풀림**

As the bolt carrier moves to the Tear, the bolt cam pin follows the path of the cam track (located in the bolt carrier). This action causes the cam pin and bolt assembly to rotate at the same time until the locking lugs of the bolt are no longer in line behind the locking lugs of the barrel extension.

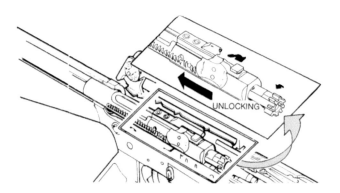

⑥ **extracting 탄피 추출**

The bolt carrier group continues to move to the rear. The extractor (which is attached to the bolt) grips the rim of the cartridge case, holds it firmly against the face of the bolt, and withdraws the cartridge case from the chamber.

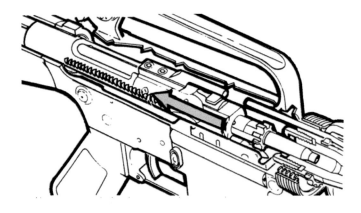

⑦ ejecting 탄피 방출/배출

With the base of a cartridge case firmly against the face of the bolt, the ejector and ejector spring are compressed into the bolt body. As the rearward movement of the bolt carrier group allows the nose of the cartridge case to clear the front of the ejection port, the cartridge is pushed out by the action of the ejector and spring

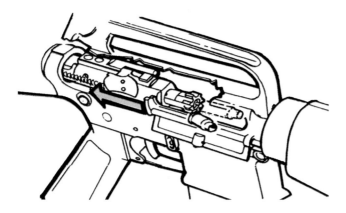

⑧ cocking 공이치기 잠김

The rearward movement of the bolt carrier overrides the hammer, forcing it down into the receiver and compressing the hammer spring, cocking the hammer in the firing position. The action of the rifle is much faster than human reaction; therefore, the firer cannot release the trigger fast enough to prevent multiple firing.

Cocking when trigger is held back during semi automatic firing.

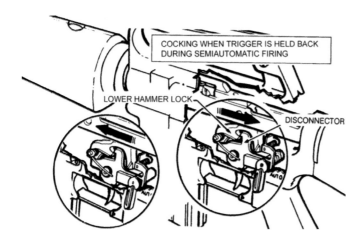

3.3 **handgun**

Revolver

Revolver puts a bullet in a cylinder instead of a magazine, and supplies bullets every time the bullets fires. It is durable, reliable, and mostly uses strong bullets. However, most of these are six or seven consecutive rounds, so the number of bullets is not enough, takes some time to reload, and the recoil is severe.

Colt M1909

examples : Colt M1909, Nagant, Webley Mk.IV.38, Colt Peace Maker

vocabulary

durable: a. 오래 견디는, 튼튼한   **pistol:** n. 권총   **chamber:** n. 방, (총의) 약실
integrate: v. 통합하다, 흡수하다
firearm: n. 화기   **buckshot:** n. 녹탄(대형 산탄)   **dozen:** n. 1다스   **bead:** n. 구슬
barrel: n. 총열, 포신
mass: a. 다량의   **telescopic:** a. 먼 곳까지 보이는   **intermediate:** a. 중간의 n. 중간
ritual: a. 의식의, 예식의 n. 의식, 관습   **caliber:** n. 직경, 구경   **ammunition:** n. 탄약
diameter: n. 직경, 지름
collective: a. 집합적인   **refer:** v. 보내다, 주목시키다   **incidence:** n. 범위, 발생률, 빈도
armored: a. 갑옷을 입은, 장갑한   **vehicle:** n. 수송수단, 탈것   **enemy:** n. 적, 원수

Pistol

Pistol is a in which the chamber is integrated with the gun, commonly referred to as a slide pistol. It is distinguished from the revolver in which the chamber is separated from the general body. the process of loading bullets into the chamber is automatically performed by a mechanical device.

Berreta M9

examples : FN Five-seveN, Desert Eagle, Clock-17, Berretta M9

ShotGun

A shotgun is a firearm that usually uses a buckshot containing dozens of beads, The shotgun has dozens of beads, so it has strong destructive power, and because of its wide range of shots, it is effective in overpowering a large number of enemies. However, compared to other guns, it is less capable of grinding and is not suitable for long-distance shooting.

Remington 870

examples : Beneli M4, Mossberg 500, Remington 870

Rifle

A rifle is a firearm with spiral rifling inside the barrel, which is used on the shoulder launched. Spiral barrel causes the bullets to rotate and, making the bullets fly more faster and farther. The advantages of this gun include excellent mass production, a high hit rate, sufficient charge bullets, and grinding power etc,.

Barret M82

examples : Barret M82, M14, FN FAL, M1 Gerand, Winchester M1873

- Sniper Rifle

The sniper rifle is a firearm used for sniping and has a telescopic view, so it is very accurate. As a sniper rifle, a bolt action method for loading a bolt with a hand is widely used.

- Assault Rifle

A sniper rifle refers to an automatic rifle that uses an intermediate-powered ammunition that has intermediate power between a combat rifle and a pistol. Currently, the ritual rifles in almost all countries are assault rifles.

- Battle Rifle

It is a rifle that uses large-caliber ammunition, can be carried, and automatically firing. Although the recoiling is strong by large diameters, it is used in modern battlefields with high stopping power to persons and destructive power.

FN FAL

- Anti-Material Rifle

 An anti-material rifle is a weapon that inherits an anti-tank rifle and is mainly used to penetrate the outer wall of an armored vehicle because the bullets are large and strong.

M60

Examples : M60, RPD, M249

- Anti-Tank Rifle

The anti-tank gun is a large-caliber gun that was used to fire enemy tanks, but it is rarely used due to its thick thickness of modern armored vehicles.

RPG-7

examples : RPG-7, PTR5, PTRD

Sub Machine Gun (SMG)

Sub Machine Guns collectively refer to automatic rifle(SMG) capable of fully automatic shooting. The advantage is that it is lighter in weight than other automatic rifle, making it easy to carry. While the incidence of failure is low due to low recoil and high hit rate, the disadvantage is that the destructive power is weak because the pistol's bullets are mainly used.

Thompson m1298

examples: Kriss Vector, FN P90, MAC-11, Thompson m1298

3.4 The part name of Magnum

Magnum is a pistol in which the chamber is integrated with the gun, and is commonly referred to as a slide pistol. It is distinguished from the revolver in which the chamber is separated from the general body.

Pistol is a firearm in which the chamber is integrated with the gun, commonly referred to as a slide pistol. It is distinguished from the revolver in which the chamber is separated from the general body. The process of loading bullets into the chamber is automatically performed by a mechanical device.

3.4.1 Magnum Specifications

The part name

① slider : The device of sliding rearwards and loaded bullets.

② recoil-assembly : The spring that slide the slider rearwards.

③ piston : A cylindrical part that reciprocates in a cylinder under fluid pressure.

④ barrel and bolt : The path which bullets go out.

⑤ magazine : A container for bullets.

⑥ trigger : A handle for shooting bullets. Pull it, bullets are fired.

⑦ locker : Lock the barrel.

⑧ remover magazine : Press it, magazine goes down.

Magnum Spec.

Data	Specifications
Type	Magnum
Manufacturer	Magnum Research
Used by	United States, Israel
Used Wars	Movies, Games
Weight/Length	1.77Kg / 269mm
Barrel length	152.4 mm
Action	Gas-operated, rotating bolt
Feed system	Detachable box magazine
Sights	Iron sights

3.4.2 The process of disassembling magnum

step 1 Remove the magazine : Press⑧ , magazine goes down.

step 2 Pull① back to make sure there's no bullet.

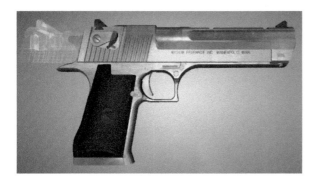

step 3 Lower locker⑦ and remove barrel.

4-1 : Pull the slider forward and remove ①.

4-2 : Pull out the recoil-assembly②.

4-3 : Pull out the piston③.

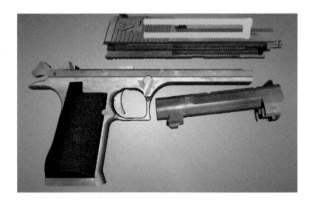

step 5 Complete disassembly.

3.4.3 Assembly process

The process of assembly is the inverse process of disassembly.

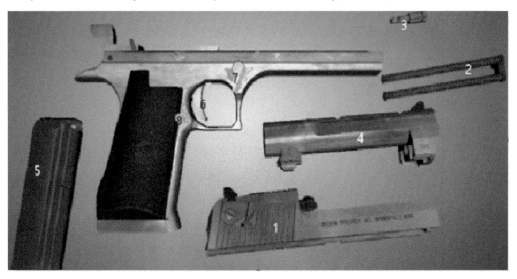

step 1 Attach the piston③, recoil-assembly② and the slider①.

step 2 Insert assembled ①②③ from the front and push it back.

step 3 Attach the barrel④ and the locker up ⑦.

step 4 Attach the magazine.

Your best records (sec)

Disassembly	Assembly	Disassembly & Assembly

3.Q Question

1. What is the Revolver ?

2. Which of the four attributes in the following examples is the wrong classification?

   ① Assault Rifle   ② Pistol
   ③ Shot Gun   ④ Laser Gun

3. Explain the 8 steps of the bullets firing process.

4. Translate the following sentence into Korean.

   4-1. Revolver puts a bullet in a cylinder instead of a magazine, and supplies bullets every time the bullets fires.

   4-2. Pistol is a pistol in which the chamber is integrated with the gun,

   4-3. A shotgun is a firearm that usually uses a buckshot containing dozens of beads, The shotgun has dozens of beads, so it has strong destructive power, and because of its wide range of shots, it is effective in overpowering a large number of enemies.

   4-4. A rifle is a firearm with spiral rifling inside the barrel, which is used on the shoulder launched.

   4-5. An anti-material rifle is a weapon that inherits an anti-tank rifle and is mainly used to penetrate the outer wall of an armored vehicle because the bullets are large and strong

5. 다음을 영작하시오.

5-1. 총알은 8단계를 거쳐 발사된다.

5-2. 전투 소총은 강한 대인 저지력과 파괴력이 있기 때문에 현대 전투에서 가장 많이 사용된다.

5-3. 자동 소총은 총알이 발사되고 자동적으로 재장전 되며 반자동 소총과 완전 자동 소총으로 분류된다.

3.N Note

3.R Reference

https://www.goarmy.mil.kr:447/goarmy/2689/subview.do

https://www.nco.mil.kr:456/nco/2283/subview.do

facebook.com/sega.svd

http://www.youtube.com/c/SegaSvd

https://ko.wikipedia.org/wiki/피스톨

https://ncs.go.kr/th03/TH0302List.do?dirSeq=122

https://ko.wikitrev.com/wiki/Assault_rifle

Chapter 4

Training and Exercise

4 Training and Exercise

4.1 Soldier's Training

Common training for individual soldiers

Common training for individual soldiers are essential training for individual soldiers to fight, survive and win in battlefiled. It has 14 tasks to do and enlisted man basically have to master all of tasks, but which reaches the required standard can be omitted. Soldiers conduct the total system of training with a combat models because all of the common tasks are related to each other.

vocabulary

conduct: v. 수행하다.   **guard post:** 경비초소
essential: a. 근본적인   **omit:** v. 빼다, 생략하다   **trainee:** n. 연습생, 훈련생
oppose: v. 반대하다   **approach:** v. ~에 가까이 가다, 접근하다
canalize: v. 어떤 방향으로 이끌다   **point-blank:** 근접 지점, 단도직입적인
markmanship: 사격술   **neutralize:** v. 중화시키다. 무효화시키다
reinforce: v. 보강하다 강화하다   **comparatively:** adv. 비교적으로, 꽤, 상당히
morale: n. 사기, 의욕   **trench:** n. 도랑, 참호   **fox hole:** n. 1인용 참호, 피난 장소
grenade: n. 수류탄   **reinforce:** v. 강화하다. 보강하다
concealment: n. 은폐, 숨김   **Protective Posture:** 보호태세
respiratory: a. 호흡기의   **exhaled:** v. 내쉬다, 내뿜다

Information collection training

Information collection training is conducted in the following way. Trainees are divided into two opposing groups and two members of friendly force will conduct security mission while the enemy tries to approach the guard post. The guards should report when they find the enemy including what, when, and where. And they should be able to canalize them into point-blank range and neutralize them with rifles and hand grenades, but capturing them is the best option.

Hand grenade attack training

Hand grenade attack has three effect.

First, it can reinforce the effectiveness of rifle fire.

Second, it forms a comparatively wider kill zone against the enemy.

Third, it makes the enemy frightened while building morale among our forces.

Hand grenade training's major targets are exposed troops, covered trench, fox hole communication trench.

Daylight movement

Daylight movement training's purpose is enable the soldiers to approach the objective promptly under the enemy's observation and fire. There are two ways to move the crawl and the rush.

The crawl has three ways: low crawl, high crawl, and applied crawl. High crawl can be used when we are provided with cover and concealment by the train, visibility is limited and when speed is required. The best way to move in open areas is rush.

Mission Oriented Protective Posture(MOPP)

Mission Oriented Protective Posture(MOPP) has five levels from zero to four. Each level specifies what equipment must be worn and how to act. The most important thing should do prior to nuclear attack is digging-in. When fallout contamination occurs, should stay in the trench wearing a mask and rain coat. Not exposing our bodies to the fall-out while stay in a covered trench is very important.

Markmanship

(Ref: https://www.logsa.army.mil/etms/data/A/026397.pdf)

The shooters who have already zeroed their rifles are eligible to daytime qualification. Who have successfully completed daytime fires can participate night time fires. Soldiers conduct fire under two types of night conditions such as illuminated and non-illuminated environment, reflecting the real battlefield situation. The minimum level of qualification for infantry soldiers are 75% in daytime and 50% in night time.

- Breath Control

As the firer's skills improve and as timed or multiple targets are presented, he must learn to hold his breath at any part of the breathing cycle. Two types of breath control techniques are practiced during dry fire.

- The first is the technique used during zeroing (and when time is available to fire a shot). There is a moment of natural respiratory pause while breathing when most of the air has been exhaled from the lungs and before inhaling. Breathing should stop after most of the air has been exhaled during the normal breathing cycle. The shot must be fired before the soldier feels any discomfort.

- The second breath control technique is employed during rapid fire (short-exposure targets). Using this technique, the soldier holds his breath when he is about to squeeze the trigger.

A. Breath control when zeroing, single target.

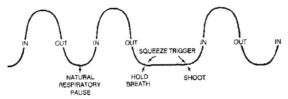

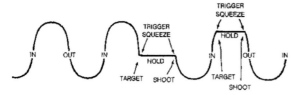
B. Breath control, firing at timed or multiple targets.

Breath Control(ref: http://impactsites2000.com/site3/data/TM9-1005-319-23.pdf)

- Firing Position

● Basic Firing Positions

Two firing positions are used during initial fundamental training: the individual supported fighting position and prone unsupported position. Both offer a stable platform for firing the rifle. They are also the positions used during basic record fire.

● Advanced Positions

After mastering the four marksmanship fundamentals in the two basic firing positions, the soldier is taught the advanced positions. He is trained to assume different positions to adapt to the combat situation

● Modified Firing Positions

Once the basic firing skills have been mastered during initial training, the soldier should be encouraged to modify positions, to take advantage of available cover, to use anything that helps to steady the rifle, or to make any change that allows him to hit more combat targets.

Aid Treatment

Key factor for successful first aid treatment is practicing the four phases of first aid action to save one's life. First, clear air passage, second stop bleeding. Third, prevent shock and continue treatment. Finally, protect wounds. To stop bleed, there are two ways. One is direct pressure and the other is using construction band. Two more points, how to use a splint for fractures and how to move the patient are should be understood.

4.2 Exercises and Training

Ul-chi Focus Lens Excercise

The purpose of Ul-chi Focus Lens Excercise is to check the overall combat readiness and necessary measures including mobilization readiness. It is not limited to MND(Military National Defence), Each department of government takes part in the exercise. This exercise to improve effective mobilization, defense industry, and civil order in the rear area.

Foal Eagle Exercise

The purpose of the exercise is to protect the facilities for combat support and combat service support in the rear area during the ROK and US combined operations in wartime. Strategic and operational echelons should pay attention to exercise more than other levels. It will be conducted by the ROK and US combined forces of corps level and above. It is also to protect critical national facilities. To develop situations, the Special Operation forces have a good opportunity to check their own OPLANs.

Regimental Combat Team training

The regimental combat team consists of an infantry regiment and some attached units such as armored units, artillery, and engineers. When organize a regimental combat team, we should consider MEIT-T. Characteristics of the regimental combat team is independence, that can perform its mission independently and be commanded by the assistant division commander.

vocabulary

fall-out: n. 부산물   **promptly:** adv. 신속히   **crawl:** v. 포복하다
concealment: n. 숨김, 은폐   **marksmanship:** n. 사격술 훈련   **eligible:** a. 적격의
qualification: n. 자격, 능력, 권한   **illuminated:** a. 비추인, 전광식을 단, 계몽된
infantry: n. 보병, 보병대   **wound:** n. 부상, 상처   **splint:** n. 부목, v, 부목을 대다
fracture: n. 부숨, 분쇄, 골절
mobilization: n. 동원   **rear:** n. 후미, 후위   **foal:** n. 새끼, v. 새끼를 낳다
echelon: n. 제형 편성, 제대   **regimental:** a. 연대의, 통제적인
artillery: n. 포, 대포, 포병   **infiltration:** n. 침투, 침입
intent: n. 의향, 목적   **maneuver:** n. 작정, 계략   **accomplish:** v. 이루다, 성취하다

Counter infiltration Operations

Operations to prepare for any military and non-military threat posed to our people, property, or national territory in order to achieve a specific purpose in a certain area during peacetime and conflict. It is divided into a counter infiltration operations and a preparation operations.

Command Post Movement Exercise(CPMX)

CPMX is the Command Post Movement Exercise for the commanders and staff officers among higher and lower headquarters while maintaining the communication network. It is conducted after completely prepared for the movement through the Rock drill. Controllers and umpires throughly prepare it by war game. Establishing a firm communication network among the echelons is the most essential part of the exercise.

Battalion Tactical training

The period of training cycle is a period from the start of the individual training to the end of battalion tactical training. The way of conducting this training is this. First, the training plan is made according to the higher commander's training intent. Officers conduct their training, teaching demonstrations, CPXs, and Command Post Movement Exercises while NCOs conduct team, squad and platton training. After that, all together conduct the Battalion field maneuver exercise. The purpose of this exercise is practicing the primary tasks and combat skills which are essential in the future battle field to accomplish the unit mission.

4.3 The part name of Shotgun

4.3.1 Mossberg 500 Specifications

The basic principle of shotgun is to attack the face rather than the point in selecting the target. The Mossberg 500 has proven to be one of the most versatile and reliable shotgun platforms available, offering a model to fit every application, and every user from our households, to law agencies, to military worldwide.

A shotgun is a firearm that usually uses a buckshot containing dozens of beads, The shotgun has dozens of beads, so it has strong destructive power, and because of its wide range of shots, it is effective in overpowering a large number of enemies. However, compared to other guns, it is less capable of grinding and is not suitable for long-distance shooting.

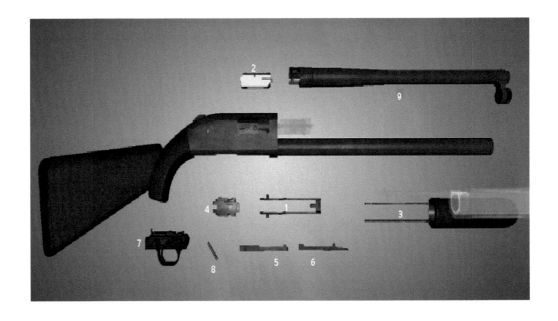

The part name

① elevator : A device that loaded bullets.

② bolt : An accessory that puts a bullet in the chamber of a rifle and takes the bullet out of the chamber.

③ action_slide : Pumping to load the bullets.

④ bolt slide : Supply bullets to a barrel.

⑤ cartridge stop : A device to stop the cartridge.

⑥ cartridge interruptor : A device that take out a bullet.

⑦ trigger_assembly : Pull it, bullets are fired.

⑧ trigger screw : Fixing the trigger.

⑨ barrel : The path which bullets go out.

Mossberg Spec.

Data	Specifications
Type	Shotgun
Manufacturer	Oscar Frederick Mossberg
Used by	United States
Used Wars	Persian Gulf War, Iraq War
Weight	2.5~3.4Kg
Barrel length	350~762 mm
Action	pump action
Feed system	5+1 to 8+1 rounds: internal tube magazine
Firing range	40~50 m
Cartridge	12 , 20 gauge

4.3.2 **The process of disassembling magnum**

step 1 Pump action_slide③ to remove the bullet and make sure the chamber is empty.

step 2 Pull action_slide③ back and fix it and remove the barrel.

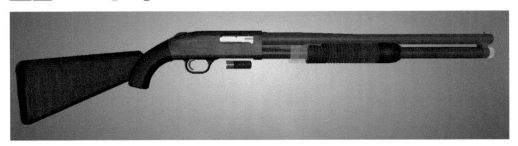

step 3 Remove trigger screw⑧ and trigger_assembly⑦.

step 4 Remove cartridge_stop⑤ and cartridge_interrupt⑥.

step 5 Remove the bolt_slide④, the bolt② and the action_slide③.

step 6 Remove the elevator①.

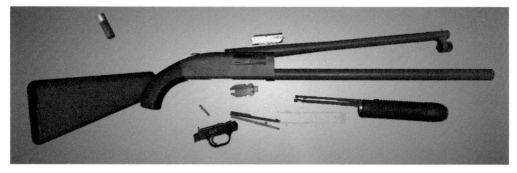

step 7 Complete disassembly.

4.3.3 Assembly process

The process of assembly is the inverse process of disassembly.

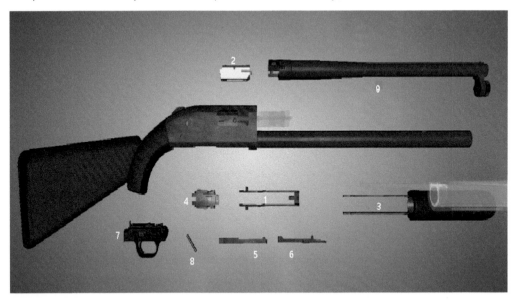

step 1 Insert the elevator① in the chamber.

step 2 Attach the bolt_slide④, the bolt② and the action_slide③.

step 3 Attach cartridge_stop⑤ and cartridge_interrupt⑥.

step 4 Attach trigger screw⑧ and trigger_assembly ⑦.

step 5 Insert action_slide③ front to back and fix it and Attach the barrel.

step 6 Pump action_slide③ to insert the bullet.

step 7 Complete assembly.

Your best records (sec)

Disassembly	Assembly	Disassembly & Assembly

4.Q   Question

1. What are the individual basic training of soldiers?

2. In the following examples, which of the four properties is the wrong classification?

    ① Ul-chi Focus Training   ② Capital Recovery Training

    ③ Regimental combat Team   ④ Counter Infiltration

3. Explain first aid steps 4.

4. Translate the following sentence into Korean.

    4-1. The purpose of the weekly movement training is to allow soldiers to quickly access the target under enemy surveillance and artillery fire.

    4-2. Information collection education is conducted in the following way.

    4-3. Each soldier's common training is essential training for each soldier to fight, survive, and win on the battlefield.

    4-4. The purpose of the Eulji Focus Lens training is to check necessary measures, including overall combat posture and mobilization posture.

    4-5. The purpose is to protect combat support and combat service support facilities in the rear area during the Korea-U.S. joint operation during the eagle training.

5. 다음 문장을 영어로 쓰세요.

5-1. 컨트롤러와 심판이 워게임으로 철저히 준비합니다.

5-2. 훈련주기는 개인훈련 시작부터 대대전술훈련 종료까지의 기간이다.

5-3. 산탄총의 기본 원리는 목표물을 선정하는 포인트보다는 얼굴을 공격하는 것이다.

4.N Note

4.R Reference

https://www.goarmy.mil.kr:447/goarmy/2689/subview.do

https://www.nco.mil.kr:456/nco/2283/subview.do

https://www.logsa.army.mil/etms/data/A/026397.pdf

facebook.com/sega.svd

http://www.youtube.com/c/SegaSvd

https://ko.wikipedia.org/wiki/산탄총

https://ncs.go.kr/th03/TH0302List.do?dirSeq=122

국방대학교 합동참모대학 WIN-WIN MILITARY ENGLISH

https://namu.wiki/w/을지훈련

https://namu.wiki/Search?q=독수리훈련

Chapter 5

Military Abbreviation

5 Military Abbreviation

(Ref:https://namu.wiki/w/군사용어 일람)

5.1 A ~ B

Abbreviation	meaning
AA	Air to Air 공대공, Assembly Area 집결지, Anti-Aircraft 대공
AAA	Anti-Aircraft Artillery 대공포
AADP	Area Air Defence Plan 지역 방공 계획
AAM	Air to Air Missile 공대공 미사일
ABC	Atomic, Biological, Chemical 화생방
ABCS	Army Battle Command System 육군 전투 지휘 시스템
ABD	Air Base Defence 기지 방호
ABM	Anti-Ballistic Missile 대탄도 미사일
A/C	Air Craft 항공기
ACSIM	Assistant Chief of Staff for Installation Management 설치담당 보좌관
ACR	Army Combat Uniform 기갑수색 연대
ADA	Air Defence Artillery 방공포병, Air Defence Area 방공구역
ADAM	Area Denial Artillery Munition 대인용 지뢰탄
ADIZ	Air Defence Identification Zone 방공식별 구역

Abbreviation	meaning
ADOZ	Air Defence Operation Zone 방공작전 구역
AF	Assault Force 강습부대
AFKN	American Forces Korea Network 한국내 미국방송
AFV	Armored Fighting Vehicle 장갑 전투 차량
AFO	Advanced Force Operations 선발 작전 부대
AGM	Air Ground Missile 공대지 미사일
AH	Attack Helicopter 공격 헬기
AIDE	부관, 보좌관
AIT	Advanced individual Tranning 후반기 주특기 교육
AIM	Air Intercept Missile 공중 요격 미사일
AKAC	Allied Crypto-graphic Operation Code or Cipher 연합작전용 암어
ALB	Air Land Battle 공지 전투
ALC	American Languqge Course 군사영어 교육
AMMO	Ammunition 실탄
ADOZ	Air Defence Operation Zone 방공작전 구역
AF	Assault Force 강습부대
AFKN	American Forces Korea Network 한국내 미국방송
AFV	Armored Fighting Vehicle 장갑 전투 차량
AFO	Advanced Force Operations 선발 작전 부대
AGM	Air Ground Missile 공대지 미사일
AH	Attack Helicopter 공격 헬기
AIDE	부관, 보좌관
AIT	Advanced individual Tranning 후반기 주특기 교육
AIM	Air Intercept Missile 공중 요격 미사일
AKAC	Allied Crypto-graphic Operation Code or Cipher 연합작전용 암어
ALB	Air Land Battel 공지 전투
ALC	American Languqge Course 군사영어 교육
AMMO	Ammunition 실탄
AO	Area of Operation 작전지역
AOE	Area of Engagement 교전 지역
AOR	Area of Responsibility 책임 지역
AOP	Aerial Observation Post 공중감시소/대공관측소

Abbreviation	meaning
AP	Ammunition Point 탄약 분배소, Armor Piercing 철갑탄, Auto Pilot
APC	Armoured Personnel Carrier(Vehicle) 장갑수송차량
AR	Armor 무기, Assault Rifle 돌격소총, Automation Rifle 자동소총
ARNG	Army Nation Guard 주방위군 육군
ARS	Auto Replying System 자동응답체계
ASM	Air to Surface Missile 공대지 유도 미사일
ASP	Ammunition Supply Point 탄약 보급소
AT	Annual Training 연례훈련, Anti-Terrorism 대테러, Anti-Tank 대전차
ATACMS	Army Tactical Missile System 육군 전술 유도탄 시스템
ATBM	Anti Tactical Ballistic Missile 대 전술 탄도 미사일
ATF	Amphibious Task Force 상륙기동부대
ATT	Army Training Test 육군훈련 시험
AV	Aviation 항공
AW	Automatic Weapons 자동화기
BCE	Battle Coordination Element 전투협조반
BCT	Basic Combat Traning 기초군사 훈련 Brigade Combat Team
BCTP	Battle Command Training Program Camp 전투지휘 훈련단
BDAR	Battlefield Damage Assessment & Repair 전장 응급 정비
BEQ	Bachelor Enlisted Quarters 독신 부사관 숙소
BL	Basic Load(Ammunition) 기본 휴대량
BM	Ballistic Missile 탄도 미사일
BOQ	Bachelor Officer Quarters 독신 장교 숙소
BOS	Battlefield Operating System 전장 관리 체계
BP	Battle Position 전투진지
BSC	Battle Simulation Center 전투 모의 센터
BTCS	Battalion Tactical Computer System 대대전술 사격 지휘 체계

5.2 C

Abbreviation	meaning
C2	Command and Control 지휘/통제
C3	Command, Control and Communications 지휘/통제 통신
C4	Command, Control and Communications and Computer 통신/컴퓨터
C/S	Chief of Staff 참모장 Call of Sign 호출부호
C4I	Command, Control and Communications, Computer and Intelligence
C4ISR	C4I and Surveillance and Reconnaissance 정보 감시 정찰 체계
CASIC	Combined All Sources Intelligence Center 연합정보 종합 상황실
CATF	Combined Amphibious Task Force 연합 상륙 기동 부대
CBRN	Chemical, Biological, Radiological and Nuclearal 화생방
CBU	Cluster Bomb Unit 확산탄
CCC	Command and Control Center 지휘통제 본부
CCIR	Commander's Critical Information Requirement 지휘관 중요첩보 요구
CCP	Communications Check Point 통신확인점
CCT	Combat Control Team 전투 통제반
CDR	Commander 지휘관
CF	Command Facility 지휘시설 conventional forces
CFC	Combined Forces Command 연합군 사령부
CFX	Command Field Exercise 지휘조 야외 기동 연습
CG	Commanding General 사령관
CIA	Central Intelligence Agency 미 중앙 정보국
CIB	Combat Infantryman Badge 전투 보병 휘장
CLF	Combined Landing Force 연합 상륙군
CLGP	Cannon-Launched Guided Projectile 레이저 유도포탄
CO	Command Officer
COMSEC	Communication Security 통신보안
COP	Command Observation Post 지휘 관측소
CSA	Chief of Staff, Army 육군참모장
CSC	Command ann Staff Course 고급지휘관 참모과정
CSOC	Combat Service Operations Center 전투근무 작전본부
CTC	Combat Training Center 전투훈련 센터

5.3 D ~ F

Abbreviation	meaning
DA	Department of the Army 미 육군성
DAIS	Defence Ammunition Information System 국방 탄약정보 체계
DAL	Defence Asset List 방어자산목록
DBA	Deep Battle Area 중심 전투 지역
DCG	Depute Commanding General 부사령관
DEFCON	Defence Readiness Condition 전추 준비 태세
DEFPAT	Defensive Patrol 방어초계
DELIIS	Defence Equipment Logistics Integrated Information System
DLIS	Defense Logistics Information System 국방 군수 정보 시스템
DMIS	Defense Material Information System 국방 물자 정보 시스템
DMZ	DeMilitarized Zone 비무장지대
DO	Duty Officer 당직장교
DOD	Department of Defence 국방부
DP	Dual Purpose 이중목적 Decision Point 결정지점
DZ	Drop Zone 투하지역
EA(ECM)	Electronic Attack 전자공격 Engagement Area 교전지역
EH	Explosive Hazards 위험성 폭발물
EHCT	Explosive Hazards Clearing Team 폭발물 처리반
EMERGCON	Emergency Condition 긴급/비상상황
EOD	Explosive Ordinary Disposal 폭발물 처리반
EPW	Enemy Prisoner of War
ERC	Engineer River Cross 공병도하
FA	Field Artillery 야전포병
FAA	Forward Assembly Area 전방 집결지
FASCAM	Family Scatterable Mines 살포식 지뢰
FDC	Fire Direction Center 화력지휘소
FE	Foal Eagle Exercise 독수리 연습
FIST	Fire Support Team 화력지원팀
FM	Field Manual 야전 교범
FO	Forward Observer 관측 장교
FS cell	Fire Support cell 통합화력 지원실
FSO	Fire Support Officer 화력지원 장교
FTX	Field Tranining Exercise 야외 훈련 연습

5.4 G ~ J

Abbreviation	meaning
GBU	Guided Bomb Unit 항공 유도 폭탄
GCA	Ground Controled Approach 지상관제 접근
GEMSS	Ground Emplaced Mine Scattering System 지상살포식 지뢰
GIS	Geographic Inforamtion System 지리정보체계
GM	Guided Missile 유도미사일
GOP	Ground Obsercation Post 지상관측소
GP	General Purpose 일반목적용, Guard Post 감시초소
GV	Grid Variation 자편각
H	Howitzer 곡사포
HA	Holding Area 대기지점
HAHO/HALO	High Altitude High Open/Low Open 고공낙하산 개방/고공강하
HAWK	Homing All the Way Killer 호크 대공미사일
HEAT	High Explosive Anti Tank 대전차고폭탄
HEI	High Explosive Incendiary 고폭소이탄
HEP	High Explosive Plastic 플라스틱 고폭탄
H-Hour	작전 개시시간
HQ	Headquarters 본부사령부
HUMINT	Human Intelligence 민간정보
HVDP	Heavy Drop 중장비 투하
ICBM	InterContinental Ballistic Missile 대륙간 탄도 미사일
ICM	Improved Capabilities Missile 개량 미사일
ID	Infantry Division 보병사단
IIR	Imaging Infra-Red 적외선 영상
ILL	Illuminating 조명탄
INS	Inertial Navigation System 관성항법 장치
IPE	Individual Protective Equipment 개인보호 장비
IR	Infrared 적외선
IRBM	Intermediate Range Ballistic Missile 중거리탄도 미사일
ITO	Intergrated Tasking Order 통합임부 명령서
JCS	Joint Chiefs of Staff 합동참모 본부
JSA	Joint Security Area 공동경비구역
JTF	Joint Task Force 합동임무 부대
JO	Joint Operation 합동 작전

5.5　K ~ M

Abbreviation	meaning
KADIZ	Korea Air Defence Identification Zone 한국방공식별구역
KATUSA	Korea Augmentation To United States Army 미육군배속한국군
KCTC	Korea army advanced Combat Training Center 과학화전투훈련단
KIT	Personal Equipment 개인장비
KR	Key Resolve 한미 연합 지휘소연습
LA	Live Ammunition 실탄
LAN	Local Area Network 근거리 통신망
LAU	Launcher Unit 발사대
Ldr	Leader
LF	Landing Force 상륙부대
LGB	Laser Guided Bomb 레이저 유도폭탄
LGM	Laser Guided Missile 레이저 유도 미사일
LMG	Light Machine Gun 경기관총
LO	Liaison Officer 연락장교
LOS	Line Of Sight 조준선
LRBM	Long Range Ballistic Missile 장거리 탄도 미사일
LST	Landing Ship Tanks 전차상륙함
MBT	Main Battle Tank 주력 전차
MC	Military Committee 군사 위원회
MCS	Maneuver Combat Traning Center 기동통제 시스템
MD	Missile Defence 미사일 방어
M-day	Mobilization -day 동원 개시일
MDL	Military Demarcation Line 군사분계선
MEPS	Military Entrance Processing Station 병무청
MG	Machine Gun 기관총
MLRS	Multiple Launch Rocket System 다연장 로켓
MOPP	Mission Oriented Protection Posture 임무형 보호태세
MOS	Military Occupational Specialy 군사특기
MOT	Mortar 박격포
MP	Military Police 군사경찰
MRBM	Middle Range Ballistic Missile
MRE	Meals Ready to Eat 전투식량
MOB	Main Operating Base 주요 작전 기지

5.6 N ~ R

Abbreviation	meaning
NAD	Not on Active Duty 예비역
NATO	North Atlantic Treaty Organization 북대서양 조약기구
NCO	Non Commissioned Officer 부사관
NFA	No Fire Area 화력금지 구역
NFL	No Fly Line 비행금지 구역
NG	National Guard 주 방위군
NP	Napalm incendiary 네이팜 소이탄
NPT	Nuclear Non-Proliferation Treaty 핵확산 금지조약
NSC	National Security Council 국가 안정보장회의
NVS	Night Vision Sight 야간 관측기
OB	Order of Battle 전투서열
OCR	Optical Character Reader 광학 문자 판독기
OCIE	Office of Compliance inspections and Examinations 전투장비지휘검열
OMR	Optical Mark Reader 광학표시 판독기
OP	Observation Post 관측소
OPCON	Operational Controls 작전 통제
OPLAN	Operational Plan 작전 계획
OPORD	Operational Order 작전 명령
PC	Personnel Command 인사사령부
PL	Phase Line 통제선
PM	Private Military Company 민간구사기업
P/O	Present Occupant 현재 병력
PRC	Portable Radio Communication 휴대용 무선 통화장비
PRI	Preliminary Rifle Instruction 사격술 예비훈련
PT	Physical Training 체력단련
QRT	Quick Reaction Team 신속대응팀
QRF	Quck Reaction Force 기동타격대
RADAR	Radio Detection and Ranging 레이더
RAPCON	Radar Approach Control 레이더 접근 관제
RECON	Reconnaissance 정찰
RFA	Restricted Fire Area 사격제한 지역
RJ	Road Junction 교차점
ROTC	Reserve Officer's Training Cops

5.7 S~X

Abbreviation	meaning
SAM	Surface to Air Missile 지대고 미사일
SATCOM	Satelite Communication 위성통신
SATS	Standard Army Training System 표준 육군 훈련 체계
SCUD	Medium/Long Range Ballistic Missile 스커드 미사일
SF	Special Force 특수부대
SHF	Super High Frequency 초고주파
SP	Start Point 출발점
SR	Special Reconnaissance 특수정찰
SRBM	Short Range Ballistic Missile 단거리 탄도 유도탄
SRT	Special Reaction Team 특수대응팀
SSBM	Strategic Submarine Ballistic Missile 전략잠수함 미사일
TAA	Tactical Assembly Area 전술 집결지
TACON	Tactical Control 전술 통제
TCP	Traffic Control Point 교통 통제소
TG	Tear Gas 최루탄
THAAD	Terminal High Altitud Area Defence 고고도미사일 방어체계
TOD	Time of Departure 출발시간
TOT	Time on Target 동시탄착 사격
TS	Team Spirit
UFG	Ul-chi Freedom Guardian 을지연습
UXO	Unexpected Ordnance 불발탄
VIP	Very Important Person
VUL	Vulcan 발칸포
WATCHCON	Watch Condition 대북정보감시태세
WG	Working Group 야전 부대 훈련
WMD	Weapons Mass Destruction 대량살상무기
X	Experiment 실험용
XO	Executive Officer 부지휘관

5.8   Sorts of Missile

TBM(Tactical Ballistic Missile), CRBM(Close Range Ballistic Missile)

Tactical ballistic missiles have the shortest range among ballistic missiles with a range of less than 300 km.

SRBM(Short-Range Ballistic Missile)

SRBM has the range of more than 300km and less than 1,000km. Most short-range ballistic missiles can carry nuclear warheads.

MRBM(Medium Range Ballistic Missile)

MRBM is a ballistic missile with a maximum range of 1,000 to 3,000 km. This range is also included in mid-range ballistic missiles, a modern classification of global ballistic missiles.

IRBM(Intermediate Range Ballistic Missile)

IRBM is a ballistic missile with a maximum range of 3,000 to 5,000 km. IRBM has a longer range than the ballistic missile MRBM or SRBM. This is shorter than ICBM, which has a range that can reach anywhere on the planet, but has a range that can be handled at the strategic level, not at the tactical level.

ICBM(Intercontinental Ballistic Missile)

ICBM refers to a ballistic missile with a range of more than 5,500 km. In other words, it is long-range ballistic missile.

SLBM(Sub-marine Launched Ballistic Missile)

It is basically the same as ICBM, but due to the nature of the launch platform, the warhead is slightly small and the power is slightly weak. However, SLBM aims to show the opponent's strategic base or such potential in the event of a nuclear war rather than a direct blow to the goal.

ASBM(Anti-Ship Ballistic Missile)

An anti-ship missile and ballistic missile specially developed to crush warships, especially aircraft carriers. Usually, the explosion of warheads and kinetic energy make aircraft carriers capable of sinking at once.

5.9　The part name of Rifle

5.9.1　Barrett M82 Specifications

A rifle is a firearm with spiral rifling inside the barrel, which is used on the shoulder launched. The barrel causes the bullets to rotate and, making the bullets fly more faster and farther. The advantages of this gun include excellent mass production, a high hit rate, sufficient charge bullets, and grinding power etc,.

This rifle is an army's personal weapon and there is a single, continuous, automatic and semi-automatic shot so on. In Korea, M-16 was self-produced by the introduction of technology in the early 1970s. In the early 1980s, the korean rifle K-2 and the Korean machine rifle K-1 were developed and powered.

The part name

① upper_receiver : The top body.

② bolt carrier : A device that moves the bolt back and forth.

③ recoil_spring : Sliding the bolt carrier backwards to forwards.

④ magazine : 10-round bullets detachable box magazine

⑤ upper_receiver pin back : A pin fix the upper_receiver at back.

⑥ upper_receiver pin middle : A pin fix the upper_receiver at middle .

⑦ bipod pin : A pin fix bipod.

⑧ bipod : A support designed to hold the front of the firearm.

Barrentt M82 specifications

Data	Specifications
Type	Rifle
Manufacturer	Barrett Firearms Manufacturing
Used by	United States
Used Wars	Gulf War, Iraq War, Somali Civil War, Kosovo War
Weight	13.5~14Kg
Barrel length	51~74 cm
Action	Recoil-operated, rotating bolt
Feed system	10-rounds detachable box magazine
Firing range	1800m
Cartridge	.50 BMG, .416 Barrett

5.9.2 The process of disassembling magnum

step 1 Remove the magazine④.

step 2 Pull the bolt carrier and Check the chamber is empty.

step 3 Remove the upper_receiver pin⑤, ⑥ and pulled the bolt detach the upper_receiver①.

step 4 Remove bolt_carrier②.

step 5 Remove the recoil_spring③.

step 6 Pull the bipod pin⑦ and remove bipod⑧.

step 7 Complete disassembly.

5.9.3 Assembly process

The process of assembly is the inverse process of disassembly.

step 1 Using the bipod pin⑦ combined bipod⑧.

step 2 Attach the recoil_spring③.

step 3 Attach the bolt_carrie ②.

step 4 With the bolt pulled attach the upper_receiver① and combine the upper_receiver pin
⑤, ⑥.

step 5 Attach the magazine.

step 6 Complete assembly.

Your best records (sec)

Disassembly	Assembly	Disassembly & Assembly

5.Q Question

Write the meaning of abbreviation.

Abbreviation	meaning
AA	
AAM	
ABC	
ABM	
AFKN	
AMMO	
AP	
ASM	
BM	
BP	
C4	
CCT	
COP	
DMZ	
GIS	
GOP	
ICBM	
IRBM	
JSA	
KADIZ	
LRBM	
MRBM	
NATO	

5.N Note

5.R Reference

https://namu.wiki/w/군사용어 일람
http://www.youtube.com/c/SegaSvd
facebook.com/sega.svd
https://ko.wikipedia.org/wiki/배럿_M82

PART II

Data Interpretation

Chapter 6

Data Interpretation

In order to become NCO, you must pass the first written examination of military officer, the second physical examination and finally the interview. The questions of the first written test are about the spacial capability, perceptual speed, language logic, data interpretation and situation judgment.

spatial capability: 공간 능력   **perceptual speed:** 지각 속도
language logic: 언어논리   **budget:** n. 예산,   **expense:** n. 돈, 비용
data interpretation: 자료해석   **situation judgment:** 상황 판단
corresponds to A: A 에 상응하다 일치 하다
vocational: a. 1.(특정 종류의) 직업과 관련된
the four fundamental arithmetic operations: 사칙 연산
effectively: ad. 1.효과적으로,   **effectiveness:** n.1.유효(성), 효과적임
competency: n. 능력   **preparation:** n. 준비,   **numerical:** a. 숫자의
suitable: a. 적합한, 적절한, 알맞은 (↔unsuitable)
relevance: n. 1.(표현 등의) 적절, 타당성; (to) 2.(필요로 하는 데이터의) 검색 능력
measure: v. 1.(치수, 양 등을 표준 단위로) 측정하다[재다] 2.(치수, 길이, 양 등이) …이다
investigating: v.조사하다, 연구하다   **synthesizing:** v. 합성하다 종합하다.

Data interpretation corresponds to mathematical ability among basic vocational skills required of office officers. Mathematical ability refers to the ability to understand the four fundamental arithmetic operations and basic statistics required in work life and grasp the meaning the chart or efficiently present the result using the chart.

It basically performs the four fundamental arithmetic operations and accurate analysis of table and graph charts is required. In addition, mathematical concept can be expressible in written and is essential for NCOs to increase tasks effectively.

It is mathematical ability that have four sub-competencies. Four sub competencies are basic computational ability, basic statistic ability, chart analysis ability and chart creating ability.

6.1   Basic Computational Ability

Basic Computational Ability is classified three level.

In-depth level NCOs perform a complex the four fundamental arithmetic operations in multi stages and correct errors in the calculation results in task.

Basic level NCOs perform a basic the four fundamental arithmetic operations to convert them to different formats and review the calculation results in task.

Low level NCOs perform a basic the four fundamental arithmetic operations like plus and minus and verify the calculation results.

Knowledge

- A concept, unit, systems of numbers.
- Types of computational techniques required for task.
- Understanding various calculation methods.
- Understanding how to present the calculation results.
- Understanding how to use the result presentation unit.

Skill

- Interpretation of numerical data.

- Perform four fundamental arithmetic operations to need in task.

- Using units suitable for calculation results.

- Present the calculation results in a different form.

- Evaluation of calculation methods.

- Verify errors of calculation results.

- Identify the relevance of the calculation result to task.

Conditions

- In case of performing calculations in task and arrange the results.

- Measure the cost of work.

- In case of investigating of customer and consumer information synthesizing of results.

- In case of preparing the budget of organization.

- In case of presenting expenses for business performance.

- In case of comparing the cost with other products.

6.2 Basic Statistical Ability

Basic Statistical Ability is classified three level.

In-depth level NCOs utilize a complex statistical techniques in multi stages and correct errors in the calculation results in task.

Basic level NCOs utilize a basic the statistical techniques to calculate the ratios and review the calculation results in task.

Low level NCOs utilize a simple the statistical techniques to calculate the average of the value and verify the calculation results.

Knowledge

- A concept of tendency.
- Understanding of basic statistical methods.
- Understanding of graph.
- Understanding basic statistics quantity and distribution.
- Types of interpretation method of statistic data.

Skill

- Representing data through calculation of frequencies, means and ranges.
- Effective represent about the calculation results.
- Chose the method to measure data.
- Evaluation of calculation method.

vocabulary

utilize: v.1.활용[이용]하다 (=make use of),　**ratio:** n. 비율
tendency: n. 1.성향, 기질; 경향 2.동향, 추세 (=trend)
relevance: n. 1.(표현 등의) 적절, 타당성; (당면 문제와의) 관련(성) ((to))
　　　　　　3.(필요로 하는 데이터의) 검색 능력

- Verify errors of calculation results.
- Identify the relevance of the calculation result to task.

Conditions

- In the case of presenting the trend of data by investigating the information of customers and consumers.
- in the case of presenting annual product sales results.
- In case of comparing task's cost with other organization.
- In case of presenting task results.
- In case of conducting a regional survey of products sales.

6.3 Chart Analysis Ability

Analysis Chart Ability is classified three level.

In-depth NCOs can synthesize the contents by synthesizing various charts encountered in task situations.

NCOs in the basic level can summarize the contents by comparing two or three charts encountered in their task situation.

Low-level NCOs look at one chart and understand the content in their task situation.

Knowledge

- Understanding the types of charts.
- Understanding how to analyze chart.
- Understanding the principle of interpretation of the title of the chart.
- Understanding visualization data.
- Understanding information acquisition method from charts.
- Understanding pros and cons each types of charts.

Skill

- Identifying the components of the charts.
- Analyzing tables, diagrams, charts and graphs
- Comparison and analysis of presented charts.
- Getting related information from charts.
- Identifying the key points of the chart.
- Identifying the relation of charts information and tasks.

vocabulary

visualization: n. 1.[U] 눈에 보이게 함[하는 힘], 시각화; 구상화(具象化)
acquisition: n. 1.습득 2.구입[취득]한 것

Conditions

- In case of interpreting the data given as charts in task process.

- In case of measuring the cost of task presented as charts.

- In case of analyzing the change table of organization's production utilization rate.

- In case of presenting customers demand according to the season in a graph.

- In case of presenting market share with competition companies in a image.

6.4 Chart Creating Ability

Chart Preparing Ability is classified three level.

High-level NCOs emphasize and present content using various charts in their task situation.

NCOs at the normal level compare and present the contents using two or three charts in their task situation.

Low-level NCOs present content using one chart in their work situation.

Knowledge

- The object of preparing charts.
- Understanding the processing of preparing charts.
- Types of charts.
- Understanding how to express using charts.
- Understanding how to express visualization.
- Types of emphasize method of key points using chart.

Skill

- Decision to transport contents using charts.
- Effective expression according to the chart types.
- Recording proper title in the chart contents.
- Summary of the main contents to be presented in the charts.
- Using exact unit.
- Identifying the size and form to deliver the contents effectively.
- Utilization of various images effectively.

vocabulary

deliver: v. 1.(물건·편지 등을) 배달하다, (사람을) 데리고 가다
2.(연설·강연 등을) 하다, (판결 등을) 내리다
3.(약속을) 지키다, (사람들의 기대대로 결과를) 내놓다[산출하다]

Conditions

- In case of submitting work results using charts.

- In case of describing the calculation results depending on the tasks purpose.

- In case of performing calculation during tasks and organizing the results.

- In case of needing the visualization of the tasks cost.

- In the case of investigating the information of the customer and the consumer and explaining the results.

6.5 Sub-machine Gun(SMG) and Rifle

6.5.1 KRISS Vector Specifications

The KRISS Vector SMG is the ideal choice for law enforcement and military seeking a controllable, compact, weapon system for close quarter combat environments. Whether for personal security or kinetic operations, the KRISS Vector SMG is able to be re reconfigured to fit the needs of a wide variety of requirements.(Ref:https://kriss-usa.com)

Kriss Vector Specification

Data	Specifications
Type	Sub-machine gun
Manufacturer	Kriss USA
Used by	United States
Used Wars	-
Weight	2.7~3.2kg
Barrel length	140, 170 mm

vocabulary

enforcement: n. 1.(법률의) 시행, 집행 2.(복종 등의) 강제 3.(의견 등의) 강조
quarter: 1/4 close quarter combat : 근접 전투
compact: a. 1.(같은 종류의 일반적인 제품보다) 소형의[간편한] 2.(공간이) 작은
kinetic: a. 1.운동의, 운동에 의해 생기는 ad. kinetically
reconfigure: v. (특히 컴퓨터 장치나 프로그램을) 변경하다
mitigation: n. 완화

The part name

① upper_receiver : The top launcher.

② upper_receiver screw 1,2,3 : three pins that fix the upper_receiver.

③ magazine : A container for bullets.

④ recoil assembly screw : A pin that fixes the recoil assembly.

⑤ recoil assembly : At the heart of every KRISS Vector is the Super V Recoil Mitigation System, which redirects recoil forces down to counterbalance the muzzle's natural tendency to rise when fired. (Ref:https://kriss-usa.com/item/vector-smg-overview/)

⑥ bolt : An accessory that puts a bullet in the chamber of a rifle and takes the bullet out of the chamber.

6.5.2 The process of disassembling Sub-machine Gun

step 1 Remove the magazine③.

step 2 Pull the bolt carrier and Check the chamber is empty.

step 3 Remove upper_receiver screw 1,2,3 ② and detach the upper receive ①.

step 4 Remove recoil assembly screw④ and detach recoil assembly⑤.

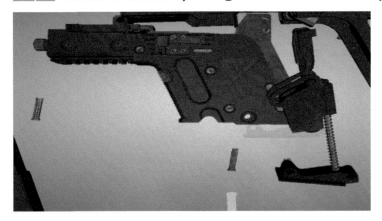

step 5 Remove the bolt ⑥ from recoil assembly ⑤.

step 6 Complete disassembly.

6.5.3 Assembly process

The process of assembly is the inverse process of disassembly.

step 1 Attach The bolt ⑥ to the recoil assembly ⑤.

step 2 Attach the recoil assembly ⑤ to the main and put the pin ④, ③.

step 3 Attach the upper receiver ① and put the pin 1,2,3 ②.

step 4 Attach the magazine ③.

step 5 Complete assembly.

6.Q Question

1. What is the mathematics ability ?

2. Which of the four attributes in the following examples is the wrong classification?
   ① Addition   ② Division
   ③ Multiplication   ④ exponential

3. What is the four ability needed data interpretation ?

4. Translate the following sentence into Korean.

   4-1. The process of assembly is the inverse process of disassembly.

   4-2. Representing data through calculation of frequencies, averages and ranges.

   4-3. Four sub competencies are basic computational ability, basic statistic ability, chart analysis ability and chart preparation ability.

   4-4. NCOs at the normal level compare and present the contents using two or three charts in their task situation.

   4-5. Data Interpretation is mathematical ability that have four sub-competencies.

5. 다음을 영작하시오.

5-1. 부사관이 되기 위해서는 군 간부 필기시험을 1차로 통과해야 한다.

5-2. 수리능력에는 지식, 기술, 업무 상황에 대한 이해가 필요하다.

5-3. 매그넘은 권총의 한 부류에 속한다.

6.N Note

6.R Reference

https://ncs.go.kr/th03/TH0302List.do?dirSeq=122

NCS 수리능력_01_교수자용.pdf

facebook.com/sega.svd

http://www.youtube.com/c/SegaSvd

https://kriss-usa.com

https://ko.wikipedia.org/wiki/반자동_권총

https://kriss-usa.com/item/vector-crb-overview/

Chapter 7

Basic Calculation Ability

7 | The example of basic calculation ability

The NCOs should be perform smoothly not only four fundamental arithmetic operations but also a complicated operations to carry out tasks effectively.

There are a lot of many examples four fundamental arithmetic operation to utilization in tasks. representative examples is as follows.

- In case of establishing of organization's budgets.
- In case of presenting the cost of tasks.
- In case of settling the receipts.
- In case of establishing the annual budgets between departments

vocabulary

not only A but also B: A 뿐만아니라 B도
representative: n. 1.대표(자) 2.(판매) 대리인, 외판원
  a. 1.(특정 단체를) 대표하는 2.전형적인
expressions: n. 1.표현, 표출 2.표정 (=look) 3.표현 (어구) 4. 표현식
bracket: n..괄호() (→angle bracket, brace) 2.(=square bracket)
exchange law: 교환 법칙, **associative law:** 결합 법칙, **distribution law:** 배분 법칙

7.1 What is four fundamental arithmetic operations?

A four fundamental arithmetic operations refer to addition, subtraction, multiplication and division about numbers or expressions. Normally a four fundamental arithmetic operations is calculated by a constant principle and method.

If +, - included in a expression, you calculate the expression in orders from the front. However, if there is brackets that combine two or more numbers, you must first calculate the number of brackets.

Addition and multiplication include commutative law, associative law, and distributive law.

commutative law : $X + Y = Y + X, \quad X \times Y = Y \times X$
associative law : $(X+Y) + Z = X+(Y+Z), \quad (X \times Y) \times Z = X \times (Y \times Z)$
distributive law : $(X+Y) \times Z = X \times Z + Y \times Z$

What do you think the answer about the following example ?

$$32 \div 2 (5 + 3) = ?$$

The answer to the above question differs from person to person.

The answer is 128 : Generally you first calculate 32/2 = 16, next calculate (5+3)=8 and last calculate 16 × 8 = 128, so the answer is 128.
The answer is 2 : Some others say multiplication symbol × is omitted. So first you calculate 2×(5+3)=16 and next 32 ÷ 16 =2, so the answer is 2.
There is no answer : There is no symbol × between 2 and (5 + 3), therefore there is a error in the expression and no answer.

7.2 Fractional number operation

Fraction is another expression of division represented by denominators and nominators, as shown in 3/4.

Can you divide the four bread to three persons?

(Ref:https://news.joins.com/articale/219869:JungAng Press)

Three bread should be divide four persons. How do you divide the three breads to four persons? It is difficult to divide three breads into four pieces from the beginning. By the way, it is much easier that first two breads is divided into two pieces having each one piece to four persons and dividing one bread into four piece having one piece per person.

By using the sum of the unit fractions, an equal distribution situation can be easily expressed. In addition to the fraction, the ratio indicating the degree of comparison, the inverse of multiplication, etc. can be expressed, and can be changed to a decimal expression.

$$1/10 = 0.1 \quad 1/100=0.01 \quad 1/1000=0.001 \quad \cdots$$

What is the length of the string that the child first had?

A child had a 30cm string. The string was first divided into half and gave to child's mother. After that, his brother asked for 3/5 of the string and gave it to him. Also, his father asked for 1/2 of the string used to kite and gave it to him. What is the length of the string that the child first had?

The answer is $30 \div 1/(1/2 \times 3/5 \times 1/2) = 200$ cm

7.3 Vedic mathematics

(Ref:http://daily.hankooki.com August 15th, 2014,
https://ncs.go.kr/th03/TH0302List.do?dirSeq=122)

"Vedic mathematics in ancient India is recognized as the origin of modern mathematics. It is called Vedic Mathematics based on the Hindu scripture Veda, and some analysts say that the calculation methods and math knowledge in Veda have developed and originated from modern mathematics. Above all, Veda Mathematics is famous for its unique four fundamental arithmetic operations method. Multiplication, subtraction and equations are also easily solved using Vedic mathematics.

In the case of addition, for example in 75+38=113, 75 is 70+5 and 38 is 30+8, and of these, the answer 13 of the single digit addition 5+8 is again identified as 10+3. Accordingly, the formula 75+38 = 70+30+10+3 = 113 is established.

$$75+38=113$$
$$75 = 70+5, 38 = 30+8$$
$$5+8 = 10+3$$
$$70+30+10+3 = 113$$

The subtraction method can be done in two ways in some cases. Usually, a multiple of 10 is used, but a certain number is added to the subtraction number to make it a multiple of 10. For example 75-38=37, add 2 to 38 to make it 40 a multiple of 10, and calculate 75-40=35. Adding the number 2 that makes 38 into 40 again, it will be the answer.

vocabulary

ancient: a. 1.고대의 (↔modern) 2.아주 오래된 n. ancientness
Hindu: n. 힌두교 신자   **scripture:** n. 경전,   **analysts:** n. 분석가
above all: 무엇보다도
famous for: ~로 유명한   **famous to:** ~에게 유명한
equations: n. 방정식

$$75-38=37$$
$$38+2=40$$
$$75-40 = 35$$
$$35+2= 37$$

Such Indian Vedic mathematics is convenient when subtracting numbers such as 100 or 1000. For example to calculate 1000-137 = 863, you first pay attention to 1 and 3 out of 137. The numbers 8 and 6 minus 1 and 3 from 9 become a hundred and ten, respectively.

$$1000-137 = 863$$
$$9-1 =8,\ 9-3= 6,\ \ 10-7=3$$

Multiplication can be used in more diverse ways. The key came from addition. For example if 17x13=221 is calculated, first the numbers 17 and 13 are considered 10+7 and 10+3. Multiply each of the ten digits to obtain 10x10=100. Subsequently, 10x7 = 70 and 10x3 = 30 are obtained by intersecting the decimal and single digits, respectively. And Multiply the digit of single to make 7x3 = 21. When all the last values obtained are added, the final value is 100+70+30+21=221."

$$17\times 13 = 221$$
$$17= 10+7,\ 13=10+3$$
$$10x10=100,\ \ 10X7=70,\ 10x3=30,\ 7x3=21$$
$$100+70+30+21=221$$

7.4   Checking Calculation

There are many wrong calculation cases in tasks. Therefore, it is necessary to go through a procedure to ensure that the calculation results are correct. Simple check methods include inverse calculation method and check of nines method(nine number elimination method).

Reverse Calculation Method

The reverse calculation check to calculate the addition as subtraction, the subtraction as addition, the multiplication as division and division as multiplication. This method is cumbersome and time-consuming, but it is widely used because of its very easy method.

For example 3+5=8. The reverse operation for this is 8-5=3 or 8-3=5.

In this way, it is calculated reverse direction to check if the calculation result is correct. Therefore, the reverse operation of addition is subtraction, and the reverse operation of multiplication is division.

One thing to note in reverse operations is that addition and subtraction should be calculated before multiplication and division.

Check of Nines Method(subtraction nine : − 9)

Check of Nines is a method of check of nines and calculating the remaining number. There are mainly three ways using check of nines.

The method is only using remainder of division by 9. Let's find out how to calculate the remainder when 34567 is divided by 9. The remainder is 7 of 34567 divided by 9. If 34567 is divided by 9, the portion is 3840, and the remainder is 7.

Check of nines method makes it easier to calculated the remainder. Simply, when the sum of the two numbers becomes 9, the numbers are discarded and the remaining numbers are the remainder. Since 3+6, 4+5 becomes 9, it is removed from 34567 and only 7 remains, so the remainder becomes 7.

$$34567 : 3+6 = 9, 4+5=9 \text{ remainder } 7$$

Another examples : addition and Multiplication

$$3456 + 723 = 4179$$
$$3456/9 = 0 , 723/9 = 3 \quad 0+3=3 \quad 4179/9=4+1+7 = 3$$

$$34 \times 72 = 2448$$
$$(30 + 4) \times (70 + 2)$$
$$30 \times 70 = 2100$$
$$30 \times 2 = 60$$
$$4 \times 70 = 280$$
$$4 \times 2 = 8$$
$$2100 + 60 + 280 + 8 = 2448$$

7.5 The part name of M4(M4 Carbine, 5.56mm)

7.5.1 M4 Carbine Specifications

The M4 carbine is a 5.56×45mm NATO machine developed in the United States during the 1980s. It is an abbreviation of the M16A2 assault rifle.

The M4 is extensively used by the United States Armed Forces and is largely replacing the M16 rifle in United States Army and United States Marine Corps (USMC) combat units as the primary infantry weapon and service rifle. The M4 has been adopted by over 60 countries worldwide, and has been described as "one of the defining firearms of the 21st century".

(REF:https://en.wikipedia.org/wiki/M4_carbine)

The part name of M4

The part name

① bolt : An accessory that puts a bullet in the chamber of a rifle and takes the bullet out of the chamber.

② bolt pin : A pin fix the bolt.

③ a firing pin : A part of an awl-shaped gun that hits the detonator of the bullet to explode.

④ bolt carrier : A device that moves the bolt back and forth.

⑤ charging_handle : A handle for loading bullets.

⑥ recoil spring : A spring to load bullets automatically.

⑦ fix lower receiver pin : A pin to combine with the main.

⑧ magazine : A container bullets.

M4 Carbine specification

Data	Specifications
Type	Rifle
Manufacturer	Colt Defense, US. Remington Arms Company
Used by	United States
Used Wars	1998 Kosovo War, Iraq War, Gaza War
Weight	2.88, 3.4Kg(With 30 rounds)
Barrel length	370 mm
Action	Gas-operated, rotating bolt
Feed system	30-round box magazine
Firing range	500m
Cartridge	5.56X45mm NATO

7.5.2 The process of disassembling M4

step 1 Remove the magazine⑧.

step 2 Pull charging handle⑤ and check the chamber is empty.

step 3 Open the fix lower receiver pin⑦ and pull down.

step 4 Remove recoil spring ⑥.

step 5 Remove the bolt carrier④ and charging handle⑤.

step 6 Remove the firing_pin③ and bolt① from bolt carrier④.

step 7 Complete disassembly.

7.5.3 Assembly process M4

The process of assembly is the inverse process of disassembly.

step 1 Attach The bolt ① in the bolt carrier④ and put the pin②.

step 2 Attach the charging handle⑤ and bolt carrier④ to the main.

step 3 Attach the recoil spring⑥ to the lower receiver.

step 4 Close up the lower receiver and push the pin.

step 5 Attach the magazine⑧.

step 6 Complete assembly.

7.Q Question

1. What is the check of nines?

2. How to divide three breads to five people?

3. What's the probability of becoming a rectangle in the following picture?

4. Translate the following sentence into Korean.

    4-1. Check of nines method makes it easier to calculated the remainder.

    4-2. Addition and multiplication include exchange law, associative law, and distribution law.

    4-3. It is difficult to divide three breads into four pieces from the beginning.

    4-4. Vedic mathematics in ancient India is recognized as the origin of modern mathematics.

    4-5. Fraction is another expression of division represented by denominators and nominators

5. 다음을 영작하시오.

5-1. 사칙연산은 덧셈, 뺄셈, 곱셈 그리고 나눗셈을 의미한다.

5-2. 총기의 분해와 조립

5-3. 구거법은 검산을 편리하게 하기 위한 계산법이다.

7.N Note

7.R Reference

https://ncs.go.kr/th03/TH0302List.do?dirSeq=122

http://daily.hankooki.com August 15th, 2014

https://ncs.go.kr/th03/TH0302List.do?dirSeq=122

https://terms.naver.com/entry.naver?docId=1188206&cid=40942&categoryId=33421

NCS 수리능력_01_교수자용.pdf

https://www.mossberg.com/category/series/500/

facebook.com/sega.svd

http://www.youtube.com/c/SegaSvd

Chapter 8

Basic Statistic Calculation

8 Basic statistic calculation

NCOs should use basic statistical techniques such as mean, sum, and frequency to grasp the characteristics and trends of data in work situations.

Many statistics can be seen around the units. When performing various tasks, it is necessary to consider in-depth what criteria to use statistical methods.

- In case of presenting the result of works.
- In case of comparing efficiency with other organizations,

8.1 What are statistics?

(Ref:https://ncs.go.kr/th03/TH0302List.do?dirSeq=122)

Statistics are numbers that reflect the state of a phenomenon by quantity and in particular, it expresses the situation of social groups in numbers.

In recent years, with the rapid development and spread of statistical methods, all collective phenomena, including natural phenomena or groups of abstract figures, are called statistics. Therefore, statistics is a field that deals with theories and methods for making wise decisions in uncertain situations and mainly has a system of data collection, classification, analysis, and interpretation.

Statistical analysis can be said to be the process of changing unknown values to known values.

Statistic Procedure

Statistic procedures are organized 4 steps. First, reduce a large amount of data to a amenable and easy-to-understand form. Second, inter group's characteristic through samples. Third, becomes aids method of decision-making. Fourth, logically certain results are extracted and checking through observable data.

8.2   Mean, Frequency and Percentage

Range

A range that is a represent tool the degree of scattering of observed values and is grasped with the maximum and minimum values and means add 1 after subtract from maximum to minimum value.

Example, If A acquires 2, 3, 4, 5, 6, 7 points, the maximum value is 7 and minimum value is 3 so A's range is 7-2+1=6.

Mean

A mean is a value that can imply the characteristics of the target group because it contains information on all observed values.

The mean has an arithmetic mean and an weighted mean.

Arithmetic mean

A arithmetic mean refers to a value obtained by adding all observed values and dividing them by the number of observed values.

Arithmetic mean of A's group = (2+3+4+5+6+7)/5 = 5.4

vocabulary

grasp: v. 1.꽉 잡다, 움켜잡다 (=grip) 2.완전히 이해하다, 파악하다
arithmetic mean: 산술 평균, weight mean = 가중 평균
symptom: n. 1.증상 2.(특히 불길한) 징후(=indication),
accumulate: v. 1.(서서히) 모으다, 축적하다 (=amass),
            2.(서서히) 늘어나다[모이다] (=build up), 어휘
variance: n. 1.변화[변동](량),   **deviation:** n. 1.일탈, 탈선 2.편차
square: 1.정사각형 (set square, T-square) 2.광장
heterogeneity: n. 이질성(異質性), 불균질(不均質)
homogeneity: n. 1.동종[동질]성, 균질성

Weighted mean

A weighted mean is calculated by multiplying each observed value by the relative weight of the data and dividing the added value by the sum of the weights.

Frequency

A Frequency refers to the degree to which an event occurs or symptoms appear, and frequency distribution is a comprehensive and clear display of such frequency in a table or graph. The frequency distribution is expressed as a number of frequency and percentage, and is divided into relative frequency distributions and accumulated frequency distributions.

Percentage

A percentage is the total quantity of 100, indicating how many of them the quantity to be expressed is. The symbol is % and 1/100 is 1%. The percentage is easy to understand using circular graphs.

Variance

A Variance is a tool that indicates to degree of spread data by specific digitization. The gabs between each observed value and the average value is squared and added, and the value is divided by the total number of times.

Example : Variance of 3, 5, 7, 9

$$Mean = 3+5+7+9 = 24 \div 4 = 8$$
$$Variance = (3-8)^2+(5-8)^2+(7-8)^2+(7-8)^2 \div 4 = 9$$

Standard Deviation

A Deviation is the square root value of variance. Standard deviation is a concept that indicates how far away it is from the mean.

Example : Variance of 3, 5, 7, 9

Mean = 3+5+7+9 = 24 ÷ 4 = 8

Variance = $(3-8)^2+(5-8)^2+(7-8)^2+(9-8)^2 \div 4 = 9$

Standard Deviation = $\sqrt{9}$ = 3

If the standard deviation is large, the data is widely spread, which means that heterogeneity is large, and if it is small, the data are concentrated and the homogeneity increases.

8.3 Five Number Summary

It is difficult to grasp the overall form of the original data only with the mean and standard deviation. Therefore, using the minimum value, maximum value, median value, bottom 25% value, and top 25% value and these are called five-number summary.

A minimum value means a value with the smallest value among the original data, and a maximum value means a value with the largest value among the data.

A median value means a value located exactly in the middle. A bottom 25% value and the top 25% value are quartered by arranging the original data in order of size. With these values, the boundary line between the upper and lower layers can be identified.

vocabulary

median: n.1.중앙값, 가운뎃값
arrange: v. 1.마련하다, (일을) 처리[주선]하다 2.정리하다, 배열하다 3.편곡하다
boundary: n. 1.경계[한계](선), 분계선

8.4 The part name of M240

M240 Specifications

The M240 machine gun is a U.S military bullet belt-like heavy machine gun using a 7.62×51mm NATO bullet. It was developed based on FN MAG machine guns.

The M240 machine gun is gradually replacing the M60 machine gun, which was the main machine gun in the U.S military.

* M240

The part name of M4

① armor magazine
② stock
③ trigger_mechanism
④ receiver
⑤ bolt assembly
⑥ drive_spring_assembly
⑦ bolt carrier

⑧ bolt
⑨ barrel
⑩ gas_regulator
⑪ 11-1: heat_shield
⑫ hand_guard
⑬ gas tube
⑭ bipod legs

M249 Carbine specification

Data	Specifications
Type	Machine Gun
Manufacturer	FN Herstal
Used by	United States, Belguim
Used Wars	Gulf War, Iraq conflict(2003~present), Kosovo War
Weight	7.5, 10kg(With 200 rounds)
Barrel length	465mm, 521mm
Action	Gas-operated long-stroke piston
Feed system	M27 linked disintegrating belt, STANG magazine
Rate of Fire	700~850
Fire range	700~800 m

8.4.2 The process of disassembling M4

step 1 Open up the cover, remove th ammo_belt, check the chamber is empty and remove the box①.

step 2 Remove the stock②, the trigger_mechanism③ and the drive_spring_assembly⑥.

step 3 Remove the bolt_group⑤⑦⑧ and disassemble it.

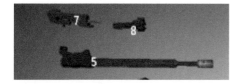

step 4 Remove the barrel⑨, disassemble the gas_regulator⑩ and remove the heat_shield⑪.

step 5 Remove the hand_guard⑫, bipod legs⑭ and the gas_tube⑬.

step 6 Complete disassembly.

8.4.3 Assembly process M240

The process of assembly is the inverse process of disassembly.

step 1 Attach the hand_guard⑫, bipod legs⑭ and the gas_tube⑬.

step 2 Attach the barrel⑨, assemble the gas_regulator⑩ and attach the heat_shield⑪.

step 3 Attach the bolt_group⑤⑦⑧ and assemble it.

step 4 Attach the stock②, the trigger_mechanism③ and the drive spring assembly⑥.

step 5 Attach the ammo_belt, the box① and close the cover.

step 6 Complete assembly.

8.Q Question

1. What is a five-number summary?

2. What is the meaning of variance and standard deviation?

3. Describe the statistical process.

4. Translate the following sentence into Korean.

   4-1. Statistics are numbers that reflect the state of a phenomenon by quantity, and in particular, the situation of a social group is expressed in numbers.

   4-2. The average contains information on all observations, so it is a value that the characteristics of the target group may be implied.

   4-3. Frequency refers to the degree to which an event occurs or symptoms appear, and frequency distribution refers to a comprehensive and clear indication of such frequency in a table or graph.

   4-4. If the standard deviation is large, it means that the data spreads widely and heterogeneity is large, and if it is small, the data is concentrated and homogeneity increases.

   4-5. The minimum value means the smallest value among the original data, and the maximum value means the largest value among the data.

5. Write down the following sentence into English.

5-1. The median value means a value located exactly in the middle. The bottom 25% value and the top 25% value are divided into four parts by arranging the original data in order of size.

5-2. If the D standard deviation is large, it means that the data spreads widely and heterogeneity is large, and if it is small, the data is concentrated and homogeneity increases.

5-3. Standard deviation is a concept that indicates how far away it is from the mean.

8.N Note

8.R Reference

https://ncs.go.kr/th03/TH0302List.do?dirSeq=122

https://ncs.go.kr/th03/TH0302View.do?fileSeq=20211220040437500qSaX5BKQ

https://ncs.go.kr/th03/TH0302View.do?fileSeq=20211220040646388NdCNkDvn

NCS 수리능력_01_교수자용.pdf

https://ko.wikipedia.org/wiki/표준편차

https://ko.wikipedia.org/wiki/분산

facebook.com/sega.svd

http://www.youtube.com/c/SegaSvd

Chapter 9

Analysis and Making Ability of Chart

9   Analysis and Making Ability of Chart

Charts can be used for various purposes, uses, and forms, and there are a wide variety of charts. Various types of charts can maximize efficiency by using them correctly depending on the purpose or situation.

9.1   Sorts of Chart

Type of Bar Chart

The bar graph is a graph showing the length of the bar to be compared by displaying the quantity to be compared, and showing the magnitude relationship between each quantity. Bar charts are used to display data details, comparisons, progress, and prescriptions.

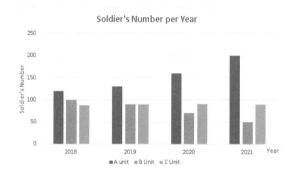

When the bars are placed horizontally, it is called a bar chart, and when it is placed vertically, it is also called a column chart.

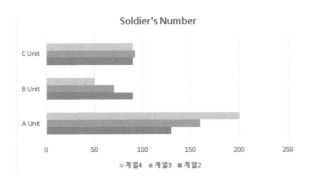

Type of Line Chart

The line(dashed line) chart is a chart indicating the change in quantity over time as the slope of the dotted line and is used to indicate correlation, including progress and comparative distribution.

The most basic use of this chart is suitable for displaying temporal trends such as changes in data by year.

When creating a line chart, the quantity is presented on the vertical axis and the name division (year, place, type etc.) on the horizontal axis, and the shape of the axis is generally L-typed. In addition, since figures are often grasped according to the height of the line, it is effective to make the scale of the vertical axis larger than the scale of the horizontal axis.

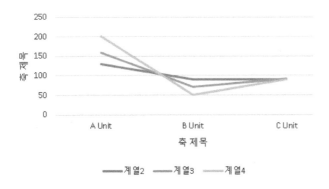

Type of Circle Chart

The circle chart is a chart created by dividing the details or the composition ratio of the contents into circles. It can be used in various ways when expressing the composition ratio for 100% of the total.

In general, when creating a circular chart, the line at 12 o'clock is used as the starting line, and it is common to draw it to the right from this point. In addition, the dividing lines are drawn in the order in which the composition ratio is large, but it is better to draw the 'other' item at the end regardless of the size of the composition ratio.

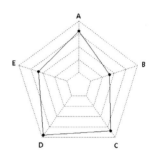

Soldier's Number

Type of Radial Chart

The radial chart is also called a spider web chart, and is a graph showing the relationship between each quantity according to the distance from the center of the circle by dividing the comparison quantity by diameter or radius, and can be used to compare each element or indicate the progress.

Type of Dot Chart

A dot chart is a chart created when two elements are placed on the horizontal and vertical axes and when you want to know where what you want to know is located. The dot chart is used to indicate the evaluation, location, and character of cities, provinces, businesses, goods, etc., as well as regional distribution.

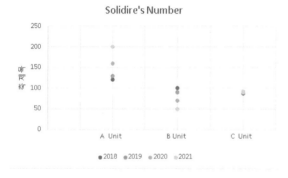

Solidire's Number

9.2 Chart Analysis Ability

9.2.1 Precautions for chart interpretation.

The level of knowledge required

In most cases, interpretation of charts does not require special knowledge. However, there is a difference in the level of knowledge, so common sense may be knowledge for some. Therefore, as a noncommissioned officer, it is necessary to generalize special knowledge into general knowledge through the acquisition of basic knowledge related to one's work.

Accurate understanding of the meaning of the data presented in the chart.

If you inadvertently interpret a given data of chart, you can expand and interpret the true meaning of the data. For example, the large number of applicants for the non-commissioned infantry department does not mean that the department selects a large number of applicants, which may be mistaken for the same thing.

The distinction between knowing and don't knowing from the chart.

It is necessary to completely distinguish between what is known and what is unknown from the data of a given diagram. In other words, it is difficult to expand and interpret the meaning from a given diagram, and a universal valid basis for sufficiently inferring one's argument based on the given diagram must be presented.

The distinction between an increase in total amount and an increase in ratio.

Even if the ratio is the same, there can be many differences in total quantity. In addition, even if there is a difference in the ratio, if the total amount is not indicated, the absolute amount cannot be evaluated based on the difference in the ratio, so a careful review is required.

Understanding percentile and a quarter rank number

Percentile refers to values divided by 100 equal parts of data arranged in order of size. For example, the 90th percentile refers to a value in which 90% of the observed values are less than or equal to that value when data are listed in order of size, and the observed value (100-90%) is greater than or equal to that value.

The quartile is a quarter of the data, and the first quartile corresponds to the 25th quartile, the second quartile corresponds to the 50th (central), the third quartile corresponds to the 75th quartile, and the rest corresponds to the 100th quartile.

9.2.2 The procedure of creating chart

Decide which chart to create

When creating a chart in the course of business performance, first, carefully review the given data to determine which chart to create using. Chart can be effective when used correctly according to purpose or situation, so deciding which chart to use should be preceded.

Decide to represent the horizontal and vertical axes

The given data should be used to determine what to represent on the horizontal and vertical axes. In general, the horizontal axis represents the name division (year, month, place, etc.) and the vertical axis represents the quantity (amount, sales, etc.), and the shape of the axis is generally L-typed.

Determine the scale size of the horizontal and vertical axes

The scale size of the horizontal and vertical axes should be determined so that the given data can be best expressed. If the size of one scale is too large or too small, the change in data cannot be well expressed, so it is desirable to determine the size of the scale that best expresses the data.

Mark the data where the horizontal and vertical axes meet

Each data is displayed on the determined axis. At this time, be careful because an accurate chart can be created only when marked accurately where the horizontal axis and the vertical axis meet.

Draw a chart according to the indicated points

Use the indicated points to actually chart. If it is a line graph, draw a chart by dividing the displayed points, and if it is a bar graph, draw a bar using the marked points to create a chart.

Indicate the title and unit of the chart

After filling out the chart, mark the unit with the title at the top or bottom of the chart.

9.3 Chart Creating Ability

Various word editors provide table and chart creating functions. In order to create a chart, you must first provide data using the table and create it a chart suitable for the purpose. In this section, we will learn how to create charts using Excel programs.

9.3.1 Creating a Bar Chart

The bar chart is a graph showing the amount to be compared by the length of the bar, comparing the length, and showing the magnitude relationship between each quantity. Let's make the next table and make it a bar chart.

① Select table in main menu and input the 5x4 data as shown the following figure.

Table. The Number of Soildier per year.				
열1 ▼	열2 ▼	열3 ▼	열4 ▼	열5 ▼
Unit	2018	2019	2020	2021
A Unit	90	110	140	200
B Unit	45	48	44	40
C Unit	170	150	120	80

② In order to changing the above table to a bar chart, select the Insertion → recommended chart → bar chart menu.

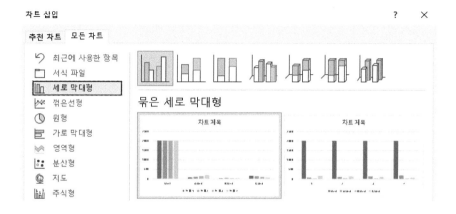

③ Select the first chart, which is a two-dimensional bar chart, among several types of bar charts and you can see the following chart.

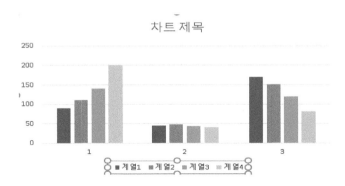

④ The components of chart are axis, subject of axis, subject of chart, data label, data table, error stick, tick lines, a legend and trend line. First of all for converting subject of chart, the title double click and change the title "The number of soldiers."

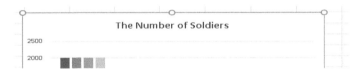

⑤ To change the legend, select the legend and press the right mouse button to click and Select Data.

⑥ Release the first legend and horizontal axis label item on screen. Press the edit button to change the legend item to "unit". As shown in the following figure, the number of members of each unit according to the legend is correctly charted.

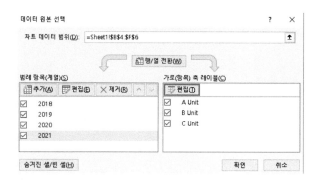

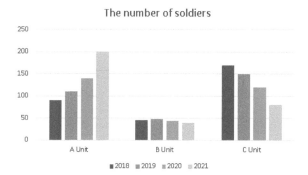

⑦ As shown in the following figure, to edit detailed items, you can select and modify each chart element.

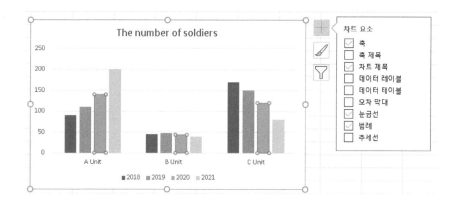

⑧ If you want to change to a different type of chart, select and click the Change Chart menu to reflect the changed chart.

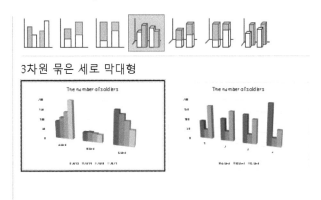

3차원 묶은 세로 막대형

9.3.2 Creating Line Chart

The line(dashed line) chart is a chart indicating the change in quantity over time as the slope of the dotted line and is used to indicate correlation, including progress and comparative distribution. It is easy to understand the change in the number of soldiers for each unit by year.

In the example above, changing the bar chart to a linear chart makes it easy to grasp the degree of change in the number of troops for each year.

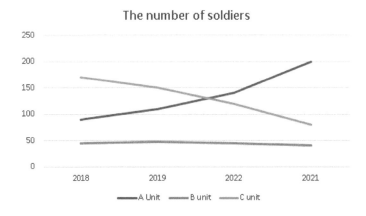

9.4 The part name of PTRS anti-tank

(Ref: https://ko.wikipedia.org/wiki/PTRS-41)

9.4.1 PTRS Specifications

The 1941 Simonov anti-tank rifle (Russian:PTRS-41) was a semi-automatic anti-tank rifle used by Soviet forces during World War II. It was created to compensate for the short-shot shooting, which was the disadvantage of the existing PTRD-41. Five 14.5 mm bullet clips were used to enable continuous shooting, making it possible to shoot quickly.

PTRS anti-tank

The part name of PTRS

① barrel
② barrel pin
③ firing pin, striker
④ gas pipe
⑤ gas pipe stopper
⑥ gas pipe stopper 2
⑦ gas system
⑧ gas system pin
⑨ bolt
⑩ recoil spring
⑪ bolt pin
⑫ cover
⑬ magazine

M249 Carbine specification

Data	Specifications
Type	Anti-tank rifle
Manufacturer	Sergei Gavrilovich Simmonov
Used by	Soviet Union
Used Wars	World WarII, Korean War, Chinese Civil War
Weight	20,93 Kg
Barrel length	1,350mm
Action	Gas-operated short-stroke gas piston
Feed system	5-round integral magazine
Rate of Fire	15 aimed shots per minutes
Fire range	800m

9.4.2 The process of disassembling M4

step 1 Move the slide back and stop it. The magazine is empty if the slide stoped.

step 2 Open down the magazine_cover and remove the clip and recoil pin and bolt carrier.

step 3 Disassembly the gas_system.

step 4 Remove the barrel.

step 5 Complete disassembly.

9.4.3 Assembly process PTRS

The process of assembly is the inverse process of disassembly.

step 1 Attach the barrel.

step 2 Assemble the gas_system and attach to the body.

step 3 Insert Clip(magazine) and Close cover.

step 4 Complete assembly.

The moment Firing

9.Q Question

다음 표를 이용하여 각 차트를 완성하시오.

	예상 비용	실제 비용	차액
담보 대출 또는 임대	₩100.00	₩1,00.00	₩0.00
통신 요금	₩54.00	₩70.00	-₩46.00
전기	₩44.00	₩56.00	-₩12.00
가스	₩22.00	₩28.00	-₩6.00
상하수도	₩8.00	₩8.00	₩0.00
케이블	₩34.00	₩34.00	₩0.00
쓰레기 수거비	₩10.00	₩10.00	₩0.00
유지 관리 또는 보수비	₩23.00	₩0.00	₩23.00
소모품	₩40.00	₩0.00	₩0.00
기타	₩0.00	₩0.00	₩0.00

1. 막대형 차트

2. 방사형 차트

3. 원형 차트

APPENDIX

Branch of the service of NCO [부사관 보직]

ref:https://www.goarmy.mil.kr:447/sites/goarmy/images/sub/2020_bintro.pdf

병과(兵科)란 군대에서 각 군인이 수행하는 주요 임무를 분류한 것으로 "군사특기"(military occupational specialty, MOS)라고도 하며, 쉽게 말해서 군인으로서의 전공이라고 말할 수 있다.

The branch of the service means classifying to performing main duties each soldiers in military, it is also called "military occupational specialty (military occupational specialty, MOS)" shortly say the major as soldier, in short, it can be said that it is a major as a soldier.

병과 구분

기본병과

- 전투병과(8) : 보병, 기갑, 포병, 방공, 정보, 공병, 정보통신, 항공
  Infantry. Armored. Artillery. Air defense. Information,
  Engineering. Signal. Air Force.
- 기술병과(4) : 화생방, 병기, 병참, 수송
  CBR. Logistics. Transportation.
- 행정병과(4) : 인사(Personnel), 군사경찰(Military Police), 재정, 공보정훈

특수병과

- 특수병과(7) : 의무(군의, 치의, 수의, 의정, 간호), 법무, 군종

Types of Branch

전투병과

- 직접 전투를 수행하는 병과로서 보병, 기갑, 포병, 방공, 공병, 정보통신, 항공 병과 등이 있다.

전투지원병과

- 전투지원병과는 직접 전투를 수행하지는 않지만 전투에 있어서 필수적인 요소를 담당하는 병과로서 병참, 수송, 병기 등이 있다.

전투근무지원병과

- 전투근무지원병과는 전투와 직접적인 관계는 없지만 군대 유지에 필요한 병과를 의미한다. 인사, 군악, 공보정훈, 군사경찰, 재정과 같은 행정병과와 의무, 법무, 군종과 같은 특수병과가 있다.

Infantry

- 육군의 여러 병과중 전투를 수행하는 육군에서 가장 많은 인원이 근무하는 핵심병과이며 지상전 투시 적 공격 및 방어는 물론 분쟁지역을 점령하여 작전을 종결
- 현대화된 보병으로서 주로 해·공군 및 기갑, 포병, 항공 등 전투병과, 전투근무지원병과 등과 긴밀한 협동과 지원 하에 전투의 승패를 결정하는 지상전투의 핵심 병과임

Armored

- 기동력화력충격력을 발휘하여 전략적작전적 수준의 결정적 작전을 수행하는 지상 작전의 종결자

Artillery

- 육군의 가장 규모가 큰 화력으로 기동부대 지원
- 가용한 화력수단을 통합하여 화력전투 수행

Defence Air

- 전투부대, 전투근무지원부대 등 중·저고도 대공방어

Information

- 적 도발 징후 조기 탐지, 경보 전파
- 적에 대한 전출처 첩보 수집 및 분석을 통한 정보생산
- 해외 파견되어 국력 홍보, 우방국과 군사교류 강화
- 아군의 정보를 보호하는 대정보 및 보안업무 수행
- 상대의 심리적 마비를 유발하기 위한 심리전활동

Engineering

- 공병은 아군의 기동을 촉진하고, 적의 기동을 방해하며, 생존성을 보장하는 병과로서 화목단결과 희생정신을 바탕으로 "시작과 끝은 우리가" 라는 모토아래 군의 전투력증강은 물론 국가안보와 국위선양에 크게 기여하는 병과

Signal

- 최신 정보통신기술을 활용 정보의 실시간 전파로 정보우위 달성 및 전장의 주도권 장악
- 사이버 공간상에 정보보호를 통한 네트워크 생존성 보장 병과

CBR

- 적의 핵 및 화생방무기 공격 시 정찰 및 인체·장비·지역 제독으로 아군의 생존성을 보장
- 화생방 테러 발생시 신속한 현장출동 및 조치로 국민의 생명을 보존
- 국가 주요행사시 화생방 분야 경호

Logistics(군수:병기)

- 육군의 지상 작전 수행을 위한 장비 / 탄약 / 수리부속 지원
- 작전 수행간 피해장비 및 물자의 정비 / 복구와 후송 및 처리

Logistics(군수:병참)

- 부대의 전투력을 유지 및 증대시키기 위하여 작전을 지원하는 기능
- 군 임무수행을 위하여 필요로 하는 물자(식량, 연료, 탄약, 축성자재 등)를 지원하여 전투력 발휘 및 작전지속능력을 보장하게 하는 일체의 활동
- 활용가치가 없는 각종 물자 및 장비의 회수, 육로 · 철도를 활용한 인원 · 물자의 수송, 목욕 · 세탁 지원 등 광범위한 업무 수행

Transformation

- 육로, 철도, 항공, 수로 등 제 수송수단을 이용한 인원 및 장비, 물자에 대한 수송지원
- 해외파병 물자 / 병력 수송지원 및 항만근무지원
- 야전부대 운전병 양성 및 수송부대 안전진단
- 철도 이동 장병 안내 및 호송 · 수송지원
- 군 작전도로 및 철도에 대한 이동관리 및 통제

Personnel

- 육군 인사근무, 제대군인 지원 업무
- 준(부)사관병 및 군무원 인사관리 및 전 신분 인사처리
- 의전 및 주요 의식행사, 상훈업무, 영현 및 전사망자 처리
- 사무관리, 온나라시스템 운영, 국가기술자격 검정 업무
- 인쇄지원, 군사우편, 해외 공무 업무
- 기록물관리, 역사관병영도서관 운영 및 관리
- 병적관리 업무, 공무원증 관리 및 민원상담 업무(육군의 74%)
- 6·25 참전용사 무공훈장 찾아주기, 모교 명패 증정 행사 등

Military Police

- 군사경찰은 군 경찰로서 법과 규정을 집행하여 군기 및 법·질서를 유지하며, 전투지원부대로써 전투부대의 작전지원을 주 임무로 하고 이를 위하여 편성·장비되며 필요한 교육·훈련을 한다.

Finance

대한민국 육군 재정병과는 육군의 살림살이를 책임집니다.

- 육군의 전투력을 강화하고 유지하기 위한 예산 획득
- 국민들이 신뢰할 수 있는 예산 집행 및 결산
- 장병들에게 급여 및 퇴직금 지급
- 시설공사, 물품구매, 용역에 대한 입찰 · 심사 · 계약체결 · 정산 등

※ 재정병과는 육군의 혈액(예산, 현금)을 공급합니다.

공보정훈

- 장병 정신교육을 통해 올바른 군인정신, 국가관, 안보관을 함양시켜 적과 싸워 이길 수 있는 정신
  적 대비태세 확립
- 홍보 및 공보활동을 통해 국민과 소통하고 신뢰 받는 강한 육군상 확립에 기여
- 문화활동을 통해 장병 사기진작, 정서 및 교양 증진 도모

의정

- 전시 의무지원 계획수립 및 전투발전 소요제기
- 평시 의무부대 병원(원무)행정, 의료관리, 의무군수, 정보작전업무
- 의무부대 전투준비태세 유지 및 교육훈련
- 국방 의무정책을 위한 법규 및 제도발전
- 미래 의무병과 발전방안 및 국제 의료지원 파병활동

The text interpretation [본문 해석]

B

1 부사관 학교

1.1 부사관

군대에서 중추 역할을 하는 부사관

부사관은 스스로 빛남으로서 명예를 추구하고 자부심을 갖는다. 부사관은 사회적 인간으로서 지켜야할 원칙을 지각하고 행동할 수 있어야 한다. 그들은 모든 일들에 있어 올바른 사고와 판단으로 건설적인 제안과 개인보다는 다른 사람을 먼저 살피는 방법을 아는 사회 공동체 의식을 견지할 수 있어야 한다. 그들은 자신의 부대와 군대에 헌신하는 전문성을 가진 유능한 인재들이다.

평생 직장으로서 안정된 직업 보장

소정의 시험(필기평가 및 인성검사, 신체검사, 체력검정, 면접평가)에 합격하면, 부사관 임관교육을 마치고 하사로 임관시 국가공무원으로 신분이 상승되고, 장기복무를 지원하여 선발되면 안정된 평생직장 보장(상사 53, 원사 55세)

최단 기간에 목돈 마련

동급 학력수준에서 일반사회와 비교할 때 군은 숙식제공, 의복비 과다지출 등이 불필요하여 부사관으로 4년 복무기간에 봉급액의 60% 저축시 최대 5천여만원 저축 가능하다.

다양한 복지 혜택으로 실질 임금 상승

독신자 숙소, 관사, 군인아파트 제공 및 군인공제회의 특별 분양 아파트 공급과 저렴한 이자의 융자 혜택으로 내 집 마련의 꿈을 조기에 달성 할 수 있다.

20년 이상의 장기 복무와 연금혜택을 통한 정년 보장

20년 이상 복무 후 전역하면 죽기전까지 연금수혜(본인사망시 70% 배우자에게 승계) 및 국립묘지 안장 등 각종 혜택 부여받고, 33년 이상 성실히 복무 후 전역할 경우 보국훈장 수혜로 국가유공자 대우 받음.

개인 전공과 능력을 발휘하는 전문 분야에서 근무

개인의 전공, 자격에 따라 전투, 기술, 행정 등 다양한 분야에서 전문화된 업무를 수행할 수 있으며, 일정자격 요건을 갖출 경우 장교, 준사관 진출 기회 부여된다.

자기 개발의 기회제공

전문대학, 사이버대학, 대학교, 대학원 진학 등 자기발전 기회 부여, 육군 주관 국가 기술 자격 검정 시험(연 2회)에 응시로 자격증 취득 기회 부여한다.

폭 넓은 자녀교육 지원

장기복무자 자녀는 중·고교 재학생 학비 전액지급, 대학 진학시 장학금 지급 및 전액 무이자로 국가에서 학비 대출 지원한다, 대도시에서 학업중인 자녀에게는 군 운영 기숙사를 제공하여 교육여건을 보장한다.

1.2 NCO의 역사와 영예 의식

1895 고종 황제 32년

부사관 시스템 시작

3단계 계급 참교-부교-정교

1945 광복군,

광복군, 4계급(참사-부사-정사-특부정사)

1946.01 국방경비대,

6계급(참교-부교-특무부교-정교-특무정교-대특무정교)

1946.12

6계급(하사-이등중사-일등중사-이등상사-일등상사-특무상사)

1949 4계급(하사-중사-상사-특무상사),

의무복무(3년)

1962.04

3계급(하사-중사-상사),

의무복무(4년), 정년(45세)

1967.02

주임상사 제도 확정 / 운용

1980.12

복무기간(장기7년, 단기4년), 정년(50세)

1989.03

4계급(하사-중사-상사-일등상사),

정년(53세)

1994.01

4계급(하사-중사-상사-원사), 정년(55세)

1995.06

직책명칭 변경(선임하사→ 행정보급관/ 업무담당관/ 부소대장)

1996.10

계급장 형태 및 부착위치 개선

2001.03

부사관 신문명칭 개정(하사관→ 부사관)

2005.01

주임원사 예우 / 운용제대 기준 설정

명예의식

① 입문의식

입교자를 축하하며, 13 · 18주간 진행될 간부화 교육과정에 대한 동기부여 및 각오를 다지기 위해 입교식 당일 야간에 해당 교육대에서 의식행사가 진행된다.

② 육탄 10용사 계승의식

위국헌신 군인본분의 귀감이 되고자 하는 부사관 교육생으로서 송악산 비둘기고지에서 장렬히 전사한 육탄 10용사의 희생정신, 충성심, 투철한 군인정신을 계승하기 위해 육탄 10용사像 앞에서 의식행사를 실시한다.

③ 탄생의식

신분화 과정 교육기간 동안의 노고를 치하하고 후보생 상호간 동기애를 고취하며 야전부대 임무수행에 대한 자신감을 배양하기 위해 실시한다.

1.3 계급

군 복무상황은 야전장교, 중대장교, 부사관, 사병(군인)으로 구분된다.

영관 장교

"군에서는 장교가 중심이다. 따라서 책임의 중요성을 인식하고 업무수행에 필요한 전문지식과 기술을 습득하여 건강한 인성을 함양하고 심신수련에 힘써야 하며, 역경 속에서도 부하직원으로부터 존경과 신뢰를 받아 적절한 판단과 행동을 취할 수 있는 통찰력과 권한을 가져야 한다. 그들을 친절하게 대하고, 법을 준수하고, 솔선수범한다." (장교의 책무 중)

장교는 현장 장교와 장군으로 나뉘어 진다. 장군은 군대에서 가장 높은 계급이며 그들의 지위는 별 휘장으로 표현된다. 준장은 군대에서 가장 낮은 계급으로 하나의 별 휘장으로 표현된다. 다음으로 높은 계급은 별 두 개 달린 소장이다. 중장은 3개의 별 휘장으로 표현되며, 4개의 별을 가진 장군 바로 아래 계급이다.

장교 계급은 소령, 중령, 대령으로 나뉜다. 그들의 "휘장은 대나무를 상징하고 대나무의 수에 따라 계급이 분류된다."

소령은 대나무 잎사귀 휘장 1개를, 중령은 2개, 대령은 3개이다. 대나무는 사계절의 푸르름, 강인한 정신, 충실함을 상징한다.

위관장교

사관급 장교는 모든 초급 위관장료를 말한다. 이들은 부사관보다는 높고 영관 장교보다는 낮다. 위관 간부의 마름모꼴은 초급 간부들이 국가를 수호하겠다는 강한 의지를 상징하며 강하고 깨지지 않는 다이아몬드 형태로 표현된다.

사관급 중 계급이 가장 낮은 사람은 사관과 동등한 대우를 받는 준위이다. 준위가 되기 위해서는 부사관 중 상사 이상의 준위에 대한 진급심사를 통과해야 한다. 위관 장교의 휘장은 하나의 노란 마름모다.

준위 계급 바로 위에는 실버다이아몬드 1개의 휘장이 있는 소위가 있다. 중위의 휘장은 2개의 은색 다이아몬드이고 대위는 3개의 다이아몬드로 자신의 지위를 나타낸다.

부사관

"NCO는 부대의 전통을 유지하고 명예를 지키는 사관이다. 따라서 그들은 자신의 임무에 정통하고, 모든 일에 솔선수범하며, 법과 질서의 준수를 감독하고, 사병들의 교육, 훈련, 내사생활을 지도해야 한다. 아울러 병사를·선도하고 안전사고를 예방하며 각종 장비와 물품 관리에 힘써야 한다." (NCO 의 의무 중)

1996년 부사관 휘장은 과거 사병 휘장 위에 휘장이 찍혀 너무 커 보이던 것에서 개정되었다. 그래서 그들의 자부심을 고취시키고 장교들의 휘장처럼 보이게 하기 위해 휘장 아래에 무궁화 팻말을 달았다.

사병

사병이란 군대를 구성하는 지위가 가장 낮은 군인을 말한다. 그들에게는 소중한 지위도 없고 현장 장교의 특별한 지식도 없고 부사관에 의한 오랜 경력과 전문성도 없다. 따라서, 원칙적으로, 사병들은 하나 이상의 부사관과 장교들 밑에 여러 명의 병사들이 모여 하나의 부대를 형성한다. 이들은 군대에서 최하위 계급이지만 동시에 가장 많은 수를 동원할 수 있는 계급이기도 하다. 보병과 포병 등은 병력의 수가 중요한 군 복무 분야에서 전투력의 대다수를 차지한다. 그들은 또한 갑옷, 공군, 해군 정비와 같은 간단한 임무에서 필수적인 구성원이다.

1.4 무기 게임 설치

병사가 소유할 수 있는 무기의 종류를 알아보고, 무기의 분해와 조립을 통해 총기에 대한 이해의 폭을 넓혀보자. 이를 위해 스마트폰으로 구동하는 무기 분해·조립 게임 설치가 필요하다.
다음 단계에 따라 게임을 설치.

1단계 : 스마트폰 배경화면에서 Play Store 앱을 실행.
2단계 : 검색창에 "weapon spred"를 입력하고 "재생" 버튼을 눌러 게임을 설치.
3단계 : 설치를 완료하면 배경화면에서 다음 아이콘을 볼 수 있다.

게임 설명

게임 화면은 아래 그림과 같이 다섯 부분으로 구성되어 있다.

파트 1 : 버튼을 클릭하면 아래와 같이 파트 2에 관련 정보가 표시.

① 게임 결과 ② 달성 ③ 무기 정보 ④ 설정 ⑤ SNS

파트 2 : 파트 1의 5가지 정보를 표시.

파트 3 : 5부에서 무기를 선택하면 무기관련이 표시.

파트 4 : 다음 3개의 게임 중 하나를 선택

① 지침 : 무기의 분해 및 조립과 관련된 버튼으로서 다음과 같은 3가지 모드가 표시

동영상 튜토리얼 : 관련 무기를 YouTube에 연동하는 모드.

분해 : 관련된 무기에 대한 분해 과정을 훈련하는 모드.

조립 : 관련된 무기에 대한 조립 프로세스를 교육하는 모드.

② 기록 교육 : 무기의 분해 및 조립 시간과 관련된 버튼으로서 다음과 같이 3가지 모드가 표시.

분해 : 관련 무기의 분해 시간을 측정하는 모드.

조립 : 관련 무기의 조립 시간을 측정하는 모드.

분해/조립 : 관련 무기를 분해한 후 조립까지 걸리는 시간을 측정하는 모드.

③ 자유모드 : 무기의 내부구조와 탄환이 발사되는 원리를 확인하고 탄환의 발사속도를 제어할 수 있다. 따라서 총알이 발사되는 속도를 조절하고 내부 구조를 볼 수 있는 두 가지 모드가 있다.

총알 발사 속도를 조절.

무기의 내부를 투명하게 만드는 것.

무기의 반대 면을 봄 .

5부 : 다양한 무기를 선택할 수 있다. 하나의 무기를 선택하면 아래와 같이 관련 무기가 표시. 현재 서비스되는 무기는 리볼버, 피스톨, 샷건, 스나이퍼 라이플, 서브머신 라이플, 아솔트 라이플, 자동 기관총, 대전차 라이플이다. 우리는 위에서 언급한 무기들 중 일부를 분해하고 조립하는 것에 대해 다음 장에서 배울 것이다.

2.1 **육군의 목표**

국가 방위 중심군으로서 육군의 주목표

① 전쟁 억제에 기여한다.

군의 존재 목적은 궁극적으로 전쟁에서 승리하여 국가를 보전하는 일이지만, 싸우지 않고 이기는 것이 최선이다.

이를 위해 우리 육군은 평소 철저한 군사대비 태세를 확립하여 전쟁이 발발 하지 않도록 억제하는데 기여해야 한다는 것을 의미한다.

② 지상전에서 승리한다.

전쟁억제에 실패하여 전쟁이 발발했을 때 우리 육군은 부여받은 임무에 따라 최소의 희생으로 단기간에 지상전에서 승리하여 전쟁종결에 기여한다는 것을 의미한다.

③ 국민 편익을 지원한다.

우리 육군이 국가시책 구현에 앞장서고 국민의 안전과 편익을 적극 지원하며 장병들에 대한 민주시민 교육을 담당하는 국민의 군대임을 의미한다.

④ 정예강군을 육성한다.

미래에 예상되는 다양한 안보위협과 첨단 정보 과학전 양상에 대비하여 우리 육군이 유비무환의 정신으로 끊임없는 정예화 선진화를 추진하여 상시 최강의 유무형 전투력을 유지해야 함을 의미한다.

육군의 3대 역할

① 보장자

전쟁억제, 작전적 신속대응, 결전방위, 안전 보장.

② 구축자

남북 신뢰형상 및 평화구축 지원, 국민의 안전지원, 국제 평화유지 및 군사외교.

③ 연결자

의무복무의 가치제고, 사회 경쟁력을 겸비한 간부육성, 과학기술 산업 경제발전 기여.

2.2 육군 조직

대통령 : 육군의 최고사령관.

국방부 장관 : 대통령의 지시를 받고 합동참모본부 의장 및 참모총장을 지휘 · 감독.

합동참모본부 의장 : 국방부 장관의 지시를 받고 전투를 주요 임무로 하는 각 복무의 작전부대를 지휘 · 감독.

육군 참모총장 : 국방장관의 명령에 따라 육군 헌병대의 지휘 · 감독을 하되, 전투를 주된 임무로 하는 각 복무의 작전부대에 대한 지휘 · 감독은 제외한다.

ROKA의 하위 조직

CDC : 수도방위사령부, ATDC : 육군 훈련 및 교육 사령부, SWC : 특수전사령부, KMA : 육군사관학교, KAAY : 영천 육군사관학교, AAC : 육군 항공사령부, APC : 육군 인사 사령부, LSC : 물류 지원 명령, AMFC : 육군 동원군 사령부, AMC : 육군 미사일 사령부, OSU : 기타 부대.

지상작전사령부, 제2작전사령부, CDC, ATEC, SWC, KMA, KAY, AOC, APC, LSC, AMFC, AMC, OSU로 구성되어 있다.

지상작전사령부가 최전방을, 제2작전사령부가 후방지역을, 수도방위사령부가 서울지역을 담당한다. 다른 부대들은 특수전, 항공작전, 지속전략 지원, 교육훈련, 예비군 엘리트주의, 행정지원 등을 수행한다.

2.3 부사관 관련 보도자료

(참고: 한국전투훈련소 보도자료. 2021.9.9)

육군은 9월 9일부터 강원 인제의 한국전투훈련소(KCTC)에서 초급 부사관 450명이 이끄는 대대를 편성해 4일 밤낮으로 전문 대항부대와 함께 훈련을 시작했다.

육군이 KCTC 훈련을 위해 초급 부사관으로 구성된 전투단을 구성한 것은 이번이 처음이다.

이번 훈련은 군 전투력의 중추이자 육군의 전투력을 이끌어갈 초보 NCO가 실제 전투경험을 통해 전투능력을 익히고 소대 전투지휘관으로서 전투지도력을 배양할 수 있도록 돕기 위해 마련됐다.

현재 각 사관학교(NCO · 포병 · 공학 · 화학 · 생물 · 방사)의 'NCO 초급리더 과정'에서 450여명의 훈련병이 훈련 중이며, 이를 지원하기 위해 80여 명의 병력이 전환에 참여해 총 530명의 병사가 초급 부사관 전투대대 아래 KCTC 특수 대항군과 함께 훈련한다.

신임 부사관은 중대급 이하 전투원이 주로 구성돼 한 번에 이틀, 잠 못 자고 나흘 동안 공격 · 방어 작전 단계에서 전투훈련을 한다.

공격용 드론으로 적을 타격하고 이를 방어하는 전술적 움직임을 구현하는 '마일스 드론 시스템'도 훈련용으로 활용됐다. 그래서 NCO는 미래의 전장과 무인 전투 시스템을 경험했다.

전투원의 안전 대책도 철저히 마련돼 있다. COVID19 차단을 위해 훈련 전부터 거리두기 4단계 수준의 고강도 방역수칙을 적용하고 있으며, 사고예방 대책으로 훈련장 곳곳에 안전요원 30여명을 가동해 응급환자 후송 및 치료체계를 갖춰 훈련을 실시하고 있다.

한편 육군은 올해 처음으로 2개 여단급 부대가 교전하는 '신규 장교 KCTC 훈련'과 '신규 부사관 KCTC 훈련'에서 '신규 장교 KCTC 훈련' 등 과학전투훈련을 활용한 실용적이고 강도 높은 전술훈련을 이어가고 있다.

2.4 무기 부품 명칭

2.4.1 리볼버 사양

권총은 한 손이나 두 손으로 다룰 수 있는 개인 소화기를 말한다. 권총은 탄환이 탄창이 아닌 실린더에 넣어지고, 발사될 때마다 실린더가 회전하여 탄환을 발사한다. 미국 서부 영화에서 그 무기를 많이 볼 수 있습니다.

그것은 내구성이 있고, 믿을 수 있고, 대부분 강한 총알을 사용한다. 다만 대부분 예닐곱 발을 연발하는 것이어서 탄환의 개수가 부족하고 장전하는 데 시간이 걸리며 반동이 심하다.

부품 명칭

① 오프너 실린더 : 뒤로 당김.

② 탄약통 : 6발.

③ 제거 탄약 : 앞으로 당김.

④ 그립 나사 : 분해 및 조립용 나사.

⑤ 그립 : 손으로 잡는 부분.

⑥ 실린더 어셈블리 핀: 핀 뽑기.

⑦ 사이드 플레이트 : 노치 커버.

⑦-1,2 : 사이드 플레이트 나사.

⑧ 노치 : 후면 노치.

⑨ 배럴 : 총열.

2.4.2 리볼버의 분해 과정

1단계 : 실린더(카트리지) 열기 : back를 뒤로 당겨 실린더를 연다.

2단계 : back를 뒤로 당겨 탄약 카트리지를 제거.

3단계 : Screw 를 돌려 그립 플레이트를 제거.

4단계 : 4-1 : Cylinder를 초기 상태로 복귀.

　　　　4-2 : 실린더 조립 핀 뽑기.

　　　　4-3 : 실린더(탄약 카트리지) 제거.

5단계 : Screw 7-1,2를 돌려 플레이트를 제거.

6단계 : 완전한 분해.

2.4.3 조립 과정

조립 과정은 분해의 역과정이다.

1단계 : 사이드 플레이트 부착.

2단계 : 실린더 조립 뭉치 부착.

3단계 : 그립 부착.

자동 소총 - M16

자동소총은 탄환이 발사된 후 자동으로 재장전되는 소총으로 반자동 사격이나 완전자동사격이 가능한 소총을 말한다. 한 번에 한 발씩 수동으로 재장전하는 소총에는 볼트 동작, 펌프 동작, 레버 동작 방식이 포함된다.

3.1 각 부분의 명칭

3.2 탄환의 사격절차

M16 볼트 어셈블리의 부품 이름

1. 링, 볼트
2. 볼트
3. 핀, 추출기
4. 핀, 스프링 이젝터
5. 스프링, 헬리컬, 압축 이젝터
6. 이젝터, 카트리지
7. 추출기, 카트리지
8. 스프링 조립체, 엑스트랙터(M16A2)
9. 스프링 조립체, EXT 추출기(M4 ND M4A1)(검은색)

절차 : 송탄 → 로딩 → 잠금 → 점화 → 잠금 해제 → 추출 → 코킹

① Feeding 송탄

볼트 캐리어 그룹이 후방으로 이동하면 버퍼 어셈블리와 결합하고 액션 스프링을 하부 수신기 팽창 압축한다. 볼트 캐리어 그룹이 탄창의 상단을 비우는 경우, 탄창 스프링은 새로운 탄알로 배치한다. 볼트의 전진 이동. 액션 스프링의 팽창은 버퍼 어셈블리 및 볼트 캐리어를 보낸다. 탄창에서 새 탄을 떼어낼 만큼의 힘으로 앞으로 송탄하게 된다.

② loading, charging 장전

노리쇠 뭉치가 앞으로 이동함에 따라 노리쇠 면은 새로운 탄환을 탄약실에 밀어 넣는다. 동시에, 추출기는 카트리지의 가장자리를 잡고, 배출기는 압축된다.

③ bolt locking 노리쇠 잠김

노리쇠 뭉치가 전진할 때 노리쇠는 상부 몸통의 가이드 채널에 있는 볼트 캠 핀으로 위치가 조정됨에 따라 가장 전진한 상태로 유지된다. 노리쇠 잠금 돌출부가 총열을 확장시키기 직전에 노리쇠 캠 핀은 가이드 채널에서 나타난다. 노리쇠 잠금 돌출부 및 총열 확장의 접촉에 의해 압력을 가함에 따라 노리쇠 캠 핀은 캠 트랙을 따라 시계 반대 방향으로, 노리쇠 잠금 돌출부를 총열 뒤의 선에서 회전하며 움직인다. 소총은 발사 준비가 된다.

④ firing 발사

반구형의 탄약실에서 공이치기가 되고 SEMI 모드에서 방아쇠는 당긴다. 방아쇠는 방아쇠 핀을 회전하여 방아쇠의 앞부분을 누르고 공이하단에 있는 노치를 해제한다.

⑤ unlocking bolt 노리쇠 풀림

노리쇠 뭉치가 Tear로 이동하면 노리쇠 캠 핀이 Tear의 경로를 따라 움직인다. 그러면 캠 핀과 노리쇠 뭉치를 노리쇠의 잠금 돌출부가 배럴 익스텐션의 잠금 러그 뒤에 더 이상 정렬되지 않을 때까지 동시에 회전시킨다.

⑥ extracting 탄피 추출

노리쇠 뭉치는 계속 후방으로 이동한다. 추출기(노리쇠에 부착됨)는 카트리지 케이스의 림을 잡고 노리쇠 면에 단단히 고정한 후 카트리지 케이스를 약실에서 꺼낸다.

⑦ ejecting 탄피 방출/배출

카트리지 케이스의 베이스가 노리쇠 면에 단단히 닿으면 추출기와 추출기 스프링이 노리쇠 본체에 압축된다. 노리쇠 뭉치의 후방 이동으로 카트리지 케이스 앞부분이 배출 포트 앞부분을 비울 수 있기 때문에 카트리지는 추출기와 스프링의 작용에 의해 밀려 나온다.

⑧ cocking 공이치기 잠김

노리쇠 뭉치의 후방 이동은 공이를 오버라이드하여 공이 스프링을 리시버 안으로 밀어 넣고 공이를 점화 위치에 고정시킨다. 소총의 동작은 인간의 반응보다 훨씬 빠르기 때문에 다중 발사를 막을 만큼 충분히 빨리 방아쇠를 풀 수 없다.

공이치기는 반자동 사격 중에는 트리거가 잠김 상태가 된다.

3.3 권총

리볼버

리볼버는 탄창 대신 탄환을 실린더에 넣고, 탄환이 발사될 때마다 탄환을 공급한다. 그것은 내구성이 있고, 믿을 수 있고, 대부분 강한 총알을 사용한다. 다만 대부분 예닐곱 발을 연발하는 것이어서 탄환의 개수가 부족하고 장전하는 데 시간이 걸리며 반동이 심하다.

권총

피스톨(Pistol)은 총과 결합된 권총으로, 흔히 슬라이드 피스톨이라고 불린다. 일반적인 몸체와 분리되어 있는 권총과는 구별된다. 탄환을 챔버에 적재하는 과정은 기계 장치에 의해 자동으로 수행된다.

산탄총

산탄총은 보통 수십 개의 구슬이 담긴 버크샷을 사용하는 화기로, 산탄총은 수십 개의 구슬이 들어있어 파괴력이 강하고, 사격 범위가 넓어 다수의 적을 제압하는 데 효과적이다. 다만 다른 총에 비해 명중률이 떨어지고 장거리 사격에는 적합하지 않다.

라이플

소총은 총열 내부에 나선형으로 홈이 새겨진 화기로 견착하여 사용한다. 나선형 총열은 총알이 회전하게 하고 총알이 더 빠르고 더 멀리 날아갈 수 있게 한다. 이 총의 장점은 우수한 양산, 높은 명중률, 충분한 장전 탄환, 강력한 파워 등이다.

- 저격 소총

저격총은 저격에 사용되는 소총으로 조준경이 좋아 정확도가 매우 높다. 저격용 소총으로는 손으로 볼트를 장전하는 볼트 동작 방법이 널리 사용된다.

- 돌격소총

저격총은 전투용 소총과 권총의 중간 위력을 가진 탄약을 사용하는 자동 소총을 말한다. 현재 거의 모든 나라의 의식용 소총은 돌격용 소총이다.

- 배틀 라이플

대구경 탄약을 사용하고 휴대할 수 있으며 자동 사격이 가능한 소총이다. 직경이 커 반동이 강하지만 사람에 대한 저지력과 파괴력이 높은 현대 전장에서 활용된다.

- 대 메털리얼(anti-material) 소총

대 메털리얼 총은 대전차소총을 계승한 무기로 탄환이 크고 강해 장갑차 외벽을 관통하는 데 주로 쓰인다.

- 대전차 소총

대전차 소총은 적의 전차에 발사할 때 사용되던 대 구경의 총이지만 현대식 장갑차의 두께가 두꺼워 거의 사용되지 않는다.

기관단총(SMG)

기관총은 완전 자동 사격이 가능한 자동 소총(SMG)을 통칭한다. 다른 자동소총에 비해 무게가 가벼워 휴대가 간편한 것이 장점이다. 반동이 적고 명중률이 높아 실패 발생률이 낮은 반면 권총의 총알이 주로 사용되기 때문에 파괴력이 약하다는 단점이 있다.

3.4 매그넘의 부품 이름

매그넘(Magnum)은 탄약실이 총과 통합된 권총으로, 흔히 슬라이드 권총으로 불린다. 일반적인 몸체와 분리되어 있는 권총과는 구별된다.

피스톨(Pistol)은 총과 결합된 권총으로, 흔히 슬라이드 권총이라고 불린다. 일반적인 몸체와 분리되어 있는 권총과는 구별된다. 탄환을 약실에 적재하는 과정은 기계 장치에 의해 자동으로 수행된다.

3.4.1 매그넘 사양

부품 이름

① 슬라이더 : 뒤로 미끄러져 총알을 장전하는 장치.

② 반동 뭉치 : 슬라이더 반동 스프링.

③ 피스톤 : 실린더 안에서 유체 압력으로 왕복하는 원통형 부품.

④ 배럴 : 총열.

⑤ 탄창 : 총알 박스.

⑥ 트리거 : 총알을 쏘기 위한 손잡이. 당기면 총알이 발사.

⑦ 잠금장치 : 발사 잠김.

⑧ 리무버 매거진 : 누르면 탄창이 분리.

3.4.2 매그넘 분해 과정

1단계 : 탄창 제거 단추를 누르고, 탄창을 분리.

2단계 : 총알이 없는지 확인하기 위해 잠금장치를 뒤로 당김.

3단계 : 하부 몸통을 회전하여 배럴을 분리.

4단계 : 4-1 : 슬라이더를 앞으로 당기고 제거.

       4-2 : 반동장치 분리.

       4-3 : 피스톤을 제거.

5단계 : 분해 완료.

3.4.3 조립 과정

조립 과정은 분해의 역과정이다.

1단계 : 피스톤, 반동-어셈블리 그리고 슬라이더를 부착.

2단계 : 조립된 부품을 앞쪽에서 끼운 후 뒤로 밀어 넣음.

3단계 : 배럴과 하부 몸통을 위로 부착.

4단계 : 탄창 결합.

4 교육과 훈련

4.1 교육

병사 개개인을 위한 공통 훈련

병사 개개인의 공통 훈련은 병사 개개인이 전장에서 싸우고, 살아남고, 승리하기 위한 필수 훈련이다. 해야 할 일이 14개이며 기본적으로 사병들은 모든 일을 숙달해야 하지만, 필요한 기준에 도달하는 것은 생략할 수 있다. 병사들은 모든 공통적인 임무가 서로 연관되어 있기 때문에 전투 모델과 함께 총체적인 훈련 체계를 수행한다.

정보수집교육

정보수집 교육은 다음과 같은 방식으로 진행된다. 훈련병들은 두 개의 상대 조로 나뉘어 적이 초소로 접근하는 동안 아군 대원 두 명이 보안 임무를 수행한다. 경비병은 적을 발견했을 때 무엇을, 언제, 어디서 발견했는지 보고해야 한다. 경비병들은 적을 유인하여 소총과 수류탄으로 사살시킬 수 있다. 하지만 포획이 최선의 선택이다.

수류탄 공격 훈련

수류탄 공격은 세 가지 효과가 있다.
첫째, 소총 사격의 효과를 강화할 수 있다.
둘째, 적에 대한 비교적 넓은 사살 영역을 만들 수 있다.
셋째, 우리 군의 사기를 높이는 동시에 적을 두렵게 만든다.
수류탄 훈련의 주요 대상은 노출된 부대에 대한, 참호의 방호, 통신 확보를 위한 참호통로이다.

임무 지향적 보호 자세(MOPP)

임무지향보호태세(MOPP)는 0에서 4까지의 5가지 레벨이 있다. 각 레벨은 어떤 장비를 착용해야 하고 어떻게 행동해야 하는지를 명시한다. 핵 공격에 앞서 해야 할 가장 중요한 일은 참호를 만드는 일이다. 낙진 오염이 발생하면 마스크와 우비를 착용한 채 참호에 머물러야 한다. 덮인 참호에 있는 동안 우리 몸을 노출시키지 않는 것은 매우 중요하다.

주간 이동

주간이동 훈련의 목적은 군인들이 적의 감시와 포격 아래 목표물에 신속하게 접근할 수 있도록 하는 것이다. 이동하는 방법은 두 가지가 있다. 포복과 돌격하는 것. 포복은 세 가지 방법이 있다: 낮은 포복, 높은 포복, 그리고 적용 포복. 높은 포복은 열차로부터 엄폐와 은폐를 제공받을 때, 시야가 제한되고 속도가 필요할 때 사용할 수 있다. 탁 트인 지역에서 이동하는 가장 좋은 방법은 돌격하는 것이다.

사격술훈련

이미 소총에 영점을 맞춘 사수들은 주간 예선을 치를 자격이 있다. 주간 사격을 성공적으로 완수한 사람은 야간 사격을 수행할 수 있다. 병사들은 실제 전쟁터 상황을 반영하듯 조명이 들어오는 환경과 무 조명 환경 등 두 가지 유형의 야간 조건에서 사격을 실시한다. 보병의 최소 자격 수준은 주간 75%, 야간 50%다.

- 호흡 조절

사수의 기술을 향상시키거나, 다수의 목표물이 줄어졌을 때, 사수는 호흡 주기에서 어떤 부분에서 숨을 참아야 하는지에 대한 법을 배워야 한다. 사격 시 두 가지 종류의 호흡 조절 기술이 실행된다.

● 첫 번째는 영점 조정 중에 사용되는 기술(그리고 샷을 발사할 수 있는 시간이 있을 때)이다. 대부분의 공기를 폐에서 내뱉고 들이마시기 전에 숨을 쉬는 동안 자연 호흡이 잠시 멈추는 순간이 있다. 호흡은 정상적인 호흡 주기 동안 대부분의 공기가 배출된 후에 멈추어야 한다. 사수가 불편함을 느끼기 전에 총격을 가해야 한다.

● 두 번째 호흡조절 기술은 급발사(단기노출표적) 시 사용되며, 사수는 방아쇠를 당기기 직전 숨을 참는다.

- 사격 자세

● 기본 사격 자세

초기 기본 훈련에서 두 가지 사격 자세가 사용 된다. 개별 지지 자세와 지지되지 않은 자세. 둘 다 소총을 발사할 수 있는 안정적인 발판을 제공한다. 그것들은 또한 기본적인 기록 사격을 하는 동안 사용되는 자세이다.

- 향상된 사격 자세

두 가지 기본적인 사격 자세에서 4가지의 기본 사격 자세를 터득한 후, 사수는 향상된 사격 자세를 익힌다. 전투 상황에 적응하기 위해 다른 포지션을 취하도록 훈련받는다.

- 변형된 사격 자세

일단 초기 훈련에서 기본적인 사격 기술을 익히면, 사수는 자세를 바꾸거나, 가능한 엄호를 이용하거나, 소총을 안정시키는 데 도움이 되는 어떤 것이든 사용하거나, 더 많은 전투 목표물을 타격할 수 있도록 변화를 주도록 권장 받아야 한다.

응급처치

성공적인 응급처치를 위한 핵심 요소는 생명을 구하기 위한 응급처치의 4단계를 실행하는 것이다. 첫 번째, 기도유지 둘째 출혈을 멈추게 하며 셋째, 충격을 예방하고 치료를 계속한다. 마지막으로, 상처를 보호한다. 출혈을 멈추는 방법은 두 가지가 있다. 하나는 직접 압박법이고 다른 하나는 지혈대를 사용하고 있다. 골절 환자의 부목법과 환자 이송법 등 두 가지 사항을 추가적으로 이해해야 한다.

4.3 훈련

을지 포커스 렌즈 훈련

을지 포커스 렌즈 훈련의 목적은 전반적인 전투태세와 동원 태세를 포함한 필요한 조치를 점검하는 것이다. 국가 방위군(MND)에 국한되지 않고, 각 부처가 훈련에 참여한다. 이 훈련은 후방지역의 효과적인 동원, 방위산업, 시민질서 향상을 위한 것이다.

독수리 훈련

이 훈련은 전시에 한미연합작전 당시 후방지역의 전투지원 및 전투 복무지원 시설을 보호하는 것이 목적이다. 전략 지휘 장교들과 작전 지휘 장교들은 다른 상황들 보다 훈련에 더 신경을 써야 한다. 군단급 이상의 한미 연합군이 지휘한다. 국가적으로 중요한 시설을 보호하기 위해서이기도 하다. 상황을 발전시키기 위해 특수작전부대는 자신들의 작전계획을 점검할 좋은 기회를 갖는다.

연대 전투단 훈련

연대전투단은 보병부대와 기갑부대, 포병, 공병 등의 부대들로 구성되어 있다. 연대 전투단을 구성할 때는 MEIT-T를 고려해야 한다. 연대전투단의 특징은 독립적으로 임무를 수행할 수 있고 부사단장이 지휘하는 독립적이다.

4.4 대침투작전

지휘조기동훈련(CPMX)

지휘조기동훈련은 통신망을 유지하면서 상·하급 사령부 중 지휘관 및 참모진을 위한 지휘소 야외 훈련이다. 록 드릴을 통해 이동에 완벽하게 준비한 후 CPMX를 실시하게 된다. 통제관과 심판이 워 게임으로 철저히 준비를 한다. 각 부대 내의 확고한 통신 네트워크를 구축하는 것이 연습의 가장 중 요한 사항이다.

대대 전술 훈련

훈련주기는 개인훈련이 시작될 때부터 대대 전술훈련이 끝날 때까지의 기간이다. 이 훈련을 수행하는 방법은 다음과 같다. 첫째, 상급 지휘관의 훈련 의도에 따라 훈련 계획을 세운다. 장교들은 훈련, 시범, CPX, 그리고 지휘소 이동 훈련을 하고, 하사관들은 팀, 분대, 그리고 소대 훈련을 한다. 이후 모두 함께 대대 야전 기동훈련을 실시한다. 이 훈련의 목적은 부대 임무를 완수하기 위해 미래의 전 투 현장에서 필수적인 주요 임무와 전투 기술을 연습하는 것이다.

4.5 샷건의 부품 명칭

4.5.1 모스버그 500 규격

산탄총의 기본 원리는 한 지점을 고르는 포인트 보다는 한 면을 공격하는 것이다. 모스버그 500은 가장 다재다 능하고 신뢰할 수 있는 산탄총 플랫폼 중 하나로 입증되었으며, 가정부터 법률 기관, 전 세계 군대까지 모든 애플리케이션과 모든 사용자에게 적합한 모델을 제공한다.

산탄총은 보통 수십 개의 구슬이 담긴 산탄을 사용하는 화기로, 산탄총은 수십 개의 구슬이 들어 있어 파괴력이 강하고, 사격 범위가 넓어 다수의 적을 제압하는 데 효과적이다. 다만 다른 총에 비해 파괴 능력이 떨어지고 장거리 사격에는 적합하지 않다.

부품 명칭

① 엘리베이터 : 총알을 적재하는 장치.

② 볼트 : 소총의 탄약실에 총알을 넣고 약실 밖으로 총알을 빼내는 부속품.

③ 액션_슬라이드 : 총알을 장전하기 위한 펌프 장치.

④ 볼트 슬라이드 : 총열에 총알을 공급한다.

⑤ 카트리지 멈춤 : 카트리지 멈춤 장치.

⑥ 카트리지 인터럽터 : 총알을 재출 장치.

⑦ 방아쇠 뭉치 : 발사 장치.

⑧ 트리거 나사 : 트리거 고정.

⑨ 배럴 : 총열.

4.5.2 매그넘 분해 과정

1단계 : 펌프 슬라이드를 눌러 총알을 제거 후 약실이 비어 있는지 확인.

2단계 : 액션 슬라이드를 뒤로 당기고 고정시킨 후 배럴을 제거.

3단계 : 트리거 나사 제거 및 트리거_어셈블리 제거.

4단계 : 카트리지 제거.

5단계 : 노리쇠를 제거.

6단계 : 엘리베이터 제거.

7단계 : 분해 완료.

4.5.3 조립 과정

조립 과정은 분해의 역과정이다.

1단계 : 엘리베이터를 약실에 삽입.

2단계 : 노리쇠 부착.

3단계 : 카트리지 부착.

4단계 : 트리거 나사 및 트리거_어셈블리 연결.

5단계 : 액션 슬라이드 앞부분을 앞에서 뒤로 삽입하여 고정한 후 배럴을 부착.

6단계 : 펌프 슬라이더를 총열에 삽입.

7단계 : 조립 완료.

5.8 라이플의 부품명

5.8.1 배럿 M82 규격

소총은 총열 내부에 나선형으로 홈이 패인 화기로 어깨에 견착하여 사용된다. 나선형의 홈의 총열은 총알을 회전하게 하고 총알이 더 빠르고 더 멀리 날아갈 수 있게 한다. 이 총의 장점은 우수한 양산, 높은 명중률, 충분한 장전 탄환, 파괴력 등이다.

이 소총은 군대의 개인 무기이며, 단발, 연속, 자동, 반자동 등이 있다. 한국에서는 1970년대 초 기술이 도입되어 M-16이 자체 제작되었다. 1980년대 초, 한국형 소총 K-2와 한국형 기관총 K-1이 개발되어 동력을 공급받았다.

요소 이름

① 상단 몸통.
② 볼트 캐리어 : 노리쇠를 앞뒤로 움직이는 장치.
③ 반동 스프링 : 볼트 캐리어를 뒤에서 앞으로 미는 스프링.
④ 탄창 : 10발 총탄 탈부착형 탄창.
⑤ 상단 몸체 고정 상단핀 : 핀이 상단 몸체를 고정.
⑥ 상단몸체 고정 중간핀 : 핀이 상단 몸체를 가운데에 고정.
⑦ 지지대 핀 : 지지대 고정 핀.
⑧ 지지대 : 화기의 앞부분을 지탱하도록 설계된 지지대.

5.8.2 매그넘 분해 과정

1단계 : 탄창 제거.
2단계 : 노리쇠 캐리어를 당기고 약실이 비어 있는지 확인.
3단계 : 상부_몸체 핀을 제거하고 볼트를 당겨 상부_몸체를 분리.
4단계 : 볼트_캐리어 제거.

5단계 : 반동_스프링 제거.

6단계 : 지지대 핀을 당기고 지지대를 제거.

7단계 : 분해 완료.

5.8.3 조립 과정

조립 과정은 분해의 역과정이다.

1단계 : 지지대 핀 사용하여 지지대 결합.

2단계 : 반동_스프링 부착.

3단계 : 노리쇠 뭉치 부착.

4단계 : 노리쇠를 당긴 상태에서 상부_몸통 부착하고 상부_몸통 핀을 결합.

5단계 : 탄창 부착.

6단계 : 조립 완료.

부사관이 되기 위해서는 1차 육군장교 필기시험, 2차 신체검사, 최종 면접시험에 합격해야 한다. 1차 필기시험의 문항은 공간능력, 지각속도, 언어논리, 자료해석, 상황판단 등이 출제된다.

데이터 해석은 부사관이 요구하는 기본적인 직업능력 중 수학적 능력에 해당한다. 수학능력이란 직장생활에서 요구되는 4대 산술연산과 기초통계를 이해하고 차트의 의미를 파악하거나 차트를 활용해 그 결과를 효율적으로 제시할 수 있는 능력을 말한다.

데이터 해석은 기본적으로 4가지 기본 산술 연산을 수행하며 표와 그래프 차트의 정확한 분석이 필요하다. 또한 수학적 개념은 서면으로 표현될 수 있으며 NCO가 효과 과제를 증가시키는 데 필수적이다.

데이터 해석은 네 가지 하위 역량을 가진 수학적 능력입니다. 4가지 하위 역량은 기본 계산 능력, 기초 통계 능력, 차트 분석 능력, 차트 작성 능력이다.

6.1 기본 연산 능력

기본적인 연산 능력은 세 가지 수준으로 분류된다.

높은 수준의 부사관은 복합 4가지 기본 산술 연산을 다단계로 수행하고 계산 결과의 오류를 수정한다.

기본 수준의 부사관은 기본 4대 산술 연산을 수행하여 이를 서로 다른 형식으로 변환하고 산출 결과를 업무에서 검토한다.

낮은 수준의 부사관은 플러스, 마이너스 등 기본 4대 산술 연산을 수행하고 계산 결과를 검증한다.

지식

- 숫자의 개념, 단위, 체계.
- 작업에 필요한 계산 기술의 유형들.
- 다양한 계산법을 이해.

- 계산 결과를 표시하는 방법을 이해.

- 결과 프레젠테이션 단위 사용 방법 이해.

기술

- 수치화된 데이터의 해석.

- 작업에 필요한 4가지 기본 산술 연산을 수행.

- 계산 결과에 적합한 단위 사용.

- 계산 결과를 다른 형태로 제시.

- 계산법 평가.

- 계산 결과의 오류 확인.

- 계산 결과와 작업의 관련성을 확인.

상황

- 과업에서 산출하여 결과를 정리하는 경우.

- 작업 비용을 측정.

- 고객 및 소비자 정보를 종합하여 조사하는 경우.

- 조직 예산을 준비하는 경우.

- 사업성과를 위한 비용 제시의 경우.

- 다른 제품과 비용을 비교하는 경우.

- 사업성과를 위한 비용 제시의 경우.

- 다른 제품과 비용을 비교하는 경우.

6.2 기초통계능력

기초통계능력은 3단계로 분류된다.

높은 수준의 부사관은 복잡한 통계 기법을 다단계로 활용하고 계산 결과의 오류를 수정한다.

기초 수준의 부사관은 업무에서 비율을 계산하고 계산 결과를 검토하기 위해 기본적인 통계기법을 사용한다.

낮은 수준의 임원은 간단한 통계 기법을 이용하여 값의 평균을 계산하고 계산 결과를 검증한다.

지식

- 경향의 개념.

- 기초 통계 방법에 대한 이해.

- 그래프 이해.

- 기초통계량 및 분포 이해.

- 통계 데이터의 해석 방법 유형들.

기술

- 주파수, 평균 및 범위 계산을 통해 데이터를 표시.

- 계산 결과에 대해 효과적으로 표시.

- 데이터를 측정할 방법을 선택.

- 계산법 평가.

- 계산 결과의 오류를 확인.

- 계산 결과와 작업의 관련성을 확인.

상황

- 고객 및 소비자의 정보를 조사하여 데이터 동향을 제시하는 경우.

- 연간 제품 판매 실적을 제시하는 경우.

- 업무의 비용을 다른 조직과 비교하는 경우.

- 과제 결과를 제시하는 경우.

- 제품 판매량에 대한 지역 조사를 실시하는 경우.

6.3 차트 분석 능력

분석 차트 능력은 세 가지 수준으로 분류된다.

높은 수준의 부사관은 업무 상황에서 접하는 다양한 차트를 종합해 내용을 종합할 수 있다.

기본 수준의 부관관들은 업무 상황에서 마주치는 두세 개의 차트를 비교하여 내용을 요약할 수 있다.

낮은 수준의 부사관들은 하나의 차트를 보고 그들의 업무 상황에 맞는 내용을 이해한다.

지식

- 차트 유형 이해.

- 차트를 분석하는 방법을 이해.

- 차트 제목 해석의 원리를 이해.

- 시각화 데이터 이해.

- 차트에서 정보 수집 방법을 이해.

- 각 차트 유형의 장단점을 이해.

스킬

- 차트의 성분을 식별.

- 표, 다이어그램, 차트 및 그래프 분석

- 제시된 차트의 비교 및 분석.

- 차트에서 관련 정보를 획득.

- 차트의 주요 포인트를 파악.

- 차트 정보와 작업의 관계를 식별.

조건들

- 주어진 데이터를 업무 프로세스에서 차트로 해석하는 경우.

- 도표로 제시된 업무추진비를 측정하는 경우.

- 조직의 생산 가동률 변화표를 분석하는 경우.

- 계절에 따른 수요를 그래프로 제시하는 경우.

- 경쟁사와의 시장점유율을 이미지로 제시하는 경우.

6.4 차트 작성 능력

차트 작성 능력은 세 가지 수준으로 분류된다.

높은 수준의 부사관들은 업무 상황에 따라 다양한 차트를 사용하여 내용을 강조하고 제시한다.

보통 수준의 부사관들은 그들의 업무 상황에서 2~3개의 차트를 사용하여 내용을 비교하고 발표한다.

낮은 수준의 부사관들은 업무 상황에서 하나의 차트를 사용하여 내용을 제시한다.

지식

- 차트의 목적.
- 준비된 차트의 처리이해 .
- 차트 유형.
- 차트를 사용하여 표현하는 방법 이해.
- 시각화로 표현하기 위한 방법을 이해.
- 차트를 사용하여 주요점의 강조 방법 유형.

스킬

- 차트를 사용하여 내용을 전송.
- 차트 유형에 따른 표과적인 표현식.
- 차트 내용에 적절한 제목을 기록.
- 차트에 표시할 주요 내용에 대한 요약.
- 정확한 단위를 사용.
- 내용물을 효과적으로 전달하기 위해 크기와 형태를 파악.
- 다양한 이미지를 효과적으로 활용.

조건들

- 차트를 사용하여 작업 결과를 제출하는 경우.
- 업무목적에 따라 산출결과를 기술하는 경우
- 업무수행 중 산출 및 결과정리를 할 경우.
- 작업 비용의 시각화가 필요한 경우.
- 고객과 소비자의 정보를 조사하고 그 결과를 설명하는 경우.

6.5 기관단총(SMG) 및 소총

6.5.1 크리스 벡터 사양

KRISS 벡터 SMG는 근접전투 환경을 위한 통제 가능한 소형 무기 시스템을 찾는 군과 법 집행 기관에 이상적인 선택이다. 개인 보안이든 운동 운영이든, KRISS 벡터 SMG는 다양한 요구사항의 요구에 맞게 재구성될 수 있다.

부품 명칭

① upper_receiver : 상단 몸통.

② upper_discrew 나사 1,2,3 : 상단 몸통을 고정하는 3개의 핀.

③ 탄창 : 총알을 담는 용기.

④ 반동 어셈블리 나사 : 반동 어셈블리를 고정하는 핀.

⑤ 반동 조립 : 모든 KRISS 벡터의 중심에는 총구가 발사되었을 때 상승하는 자연적인 경향을 균형을 맞추기 위해 반동력을 아래로 돌려주는 슈퍼 V 반동 완화 시스템.

⑥ 볼트 : 소총의 약실에 총알을 넣고 약실 밖으로 총알을 빼내는 부속품.

6.5.2 크리스 분해 과정

1단계 : 탄창 제거.

2단계 : 노리쇠 뭉치를 당기고 약실이 비어 있는지 확인.

3단계 : 상부_몸통 나사 1,2,3를 제거하고 상부 몸통을 분리한다.

4단계 : 반동 어셈블리 나사 제거 및 반동 어셈블리 분리.

5단계 : 노리쇠를 반동 어셈블리에서 제거.

6단계 : 분해 완료.

6.5.3 조립 과정

조립 과정은 분해의 역과정이다.

1단계 : 볼트를 반동 어셈블리에 부착.

2단계 : 반동 어셈블리를 몸통에 부착.

3단계 : 상부 몸통을 부착하고 핀 1,2,3을 끼움.

5단계 : 탄창 결합.

6단계 : 조립 완료.

7 기본 연산의 예

부사관들은 4대 산술 연산뿐만 아니라 멀티플렉스 연산까지 원활히 수행해 업무를 효과적으로 수행해야 한다.

과제에서 활용하기 위한 4가지 기본적인 산술 연산을 예로 많이 들 수 있. 대표적인 예는 다음과 같다.

- 조직의 예산을 수립하는 경우.
- 업무추진비를 제시할 경우.
- 영수증을 정산하는 경우.
- 부서 간 연간 예산 수립하는 경우.

7.1 사칙 연산은 무엇인가?

사칙 연산은 숫자나 식에 대한 더하기, 빼기, 멀티플렉스, 나누기를 의미한다. 일반적으로 사칙 연산은 일정한 원리와 방법에 의해 계산된다.

식에 +, -가 포함되어 있으면 앞에서부터 순서대로 식을 계산한다. 그러나 두 개 이상의 숫자를 결합한 대괄호가 있으면 먼저 대괄호 수를 계산해야 한다.

덧셈과 곱셈에는 교환법, 연관법, 분배법 등이 포함된다.

교환법칙: $X + Y = Y + X$, $X \times Y = Y \times X$

연관법칙 : $(X+Y) + Z = X+(Y+Z)$, $(X \times Y) \times Z = X \times (Y \times Z)$

분포 법칙 : $(X+Y) \times Z = X \times Z + Y \times Z$

다음 예에 대한 답이 무엇이라고 생각합니까?

$32 \div 2 (5 + 3) = ?$

위의 질문에 대한 답은 사람마다 다르다.

답은 128이다. 일반적으로 32/2 = 16을 먼저 계산한 다음 (5+3)=8을 계산하고 마지막으로 16×8 = 128을 계산하므로 답은 128입니다.

정답은 2 : 다른 사람들은 멀티플렉스 기호 $\times$가 생략되었다고 말한다. 그래서 먼저 $2 \times (5+3)=16$을 계산하고 그 다음에 32×16=2를 계산하면 답은 2이다.

답이 없다: 2와 (5 + 3) 사이에 기호 ×가 없으므로 식에 오류가 있고 답이 없다.

7.2   분수 연산

분수는 3/4에서 볼 수 있듯이 분모와 지명자로 대표되는 나눗셈의 또 다른 표현이다.

빵 네 개를 세 사람에게 나누어 줄 수 있나요?

(참조:https://news.joins.com/articale/219869:중앙언론)

빵 세 개를 네 명씩 나눠야 합니다. 빵 세 개를 네 사람에게 어떻게 나누나요? 처음부터 세 개의 빵을 네 조각으로 나누는 것은 어렵습니다. 그러므로 처음 두 개의 빵을 두 조각으로 나누어 각각 4인 1조각을 가지고, 한 빵을 4조각으로 나누는 것은 훨씬 쉽다.

단위분수의 합을 사용하여 균등분포 상황을 쉽게 표현할 수 있습니다. 분수 외에 비교 정도, 곱셈의 역수 등을 나타내는 비율도 표현할 수 있고, 십진식으로 바꿀 수 있다.

1/10 = 0.1 1/100=0.01 1/1000=0.001 …

아이가 처음 가지고 있던 끈의 길이가 어떻게 되나요?

한 아이는 30cm의 끈을 가지고 있었습니다. 그 끈은 처음에 반으로 나누어 아이의 엄마에게 주어졌다. 그 후, 그의 형이 끈의 5분의 3을 요구하여 그에게 주었습니다. 또한, 그의 아버지는 연에 사용되는 끈의 1/2을 요구했고 그것을 그에게 주었습니다. 아이가 처음 가지고 있던 끈의 길이가 어떻게 되나요?

답은 30×3/5×1/2 = 200cm입니다.

7.3   베다 수학

(참고 자료:http://daily.hankooki.com 2014년 8월 15일

https://ncs.go.kr/th03/TH0302List.do?dirSeq=122)

"고대 인도의 베다 수학은 현대 수학의 기원으로 인식되고 있습니다. 힌두교 경전 베다(Veda)를 바탕으로 베다수학이라고 불리는데, 베다의 계산법과 수학 지식이 발달해 현대 수학에서 유래했다는 분

석도 있다. 무엇보다 베다 수학은 독특한 사칙 연산법으로 유명하다. 곱셈, 뺄셈, 방정식도 베다 수학을 이용해 쉽게 풀 수 있다.

예를 들어, 75+38=127에서 75는 70+5, 38은 30+8이며, 이 중 한 자리 덧셈 5+8의 13은 다시 10+3으로 식별됩니다. 따라서 공식 75+38 = 70+30+10+3 = 113이 성립한다.

75+38=113 , 75 = 70+5, 38 = 30+8, 5+8 = 10+3, 70+30+10+3 = 113

뺄셈 방법은 경우에 따라 두 가지 방법으로 할 수 있다. 보통 10의 배수가 사용되지만, 10의 배수로 만들기 위해 특정 숫자를 빼기 숫자에 더한다. 예를 들어 75-38=37의 경우, 2에 38을 더하면 40이 10의 배수로 되고 75-40=35를 계산합니다. 38을 다시 40으로 만드는 숫자 2를 더하면 답이 될 것이다.

75-38=37, 38+2=40, 75-40 = 35, 35+2= 37

이러한 인도의 베다 수학은 100이나 1000 같은 숫자를 뺄 때 편리합니다. 예를 들어, 1000-137 = 863을 계산하려면 137개 중 1과 3에 주목해야 합니다. 숫자 8과 6에서 9를 뺀 1과 3은 각각 100과 10이 된다.

1000-137 = 863, 9-1 =8, 9-3= 6, 10-7=3

곱셈은 더 다양한 방법으로 사용될 수 있다. 핵심은 덧셈에서 나왔다. 예를 들어, 17x13=221이 계산되면 먼저 숫자 17과 13은 10+7과 10+3으로 간주됩니다. 각 10자리를 곱하여 10x10=100을 구한다. 이어서 10x7 = 70과 10x3 = 30은 각각 소수점과 한 자리수를 교차시켜 구한다. 그리고 싱글의 숫자를 곱하면 7x3 = 21이 된다. 마지막으로 얻은 값을 모두 더하면 최종 값은 100+70+30+21=221이다.

$17 \times 13 = 221$, 17= 10+7, 13=10+3,

10x10=100, 10X7=70, 10x3=30, 7x3=21, 100+70+30+21=221

7.5 M4의 부품명(M4 카빈, 5.56 mm)

7.5.1 M4 카빈 사양

M4 카빈은 1980년대에 미국에서 개발된 5.56×45mm NATO 총이다. M16A2 돌격소총의 줄임말이다.

M4는 미국 육군에 의해 광범위하게 사용되고 있으며, 주요 보병 무기와 서비스 소총으로서 미국 육군과 미국 해병대 전투부대의 M16 소총을 대체하고 있다. M4는 전 세계 60개국 이상에서 채택되었으며, "21세기의 대표적인 총기 중 하나"로 묘사되고 있다.

① 볼트 : 소총의 챔버에 총알을 넣고 챔버 밖으로 총알을 빼내는 부속품.
② 볼트 핀 : 핀은 볼트를 고정한다.
③ 공이 : 송곳 모양의 총의 일부가 총알의 기폭장치를 쳐서 폭발하는 것이다.
④ 볼트 캐리어 : 볼트를 앞뒤로 움직이는 장치이다.
⑤ 장착 핸들 : 총알을 장착하기위한 핸들이다.
⑥ 반동 스프링 : 탄환을 자동으로 장전하는 스프링이다.
⑦ 하부 몸통 핀 고정 : 메인과 결합할 핀.
⑧ 탄창 : 총알통.

7.5.2 M4의 분해 과정

1단계 : 탄창 제거
2단계 : 장착 손잡이를 당기고 약실이 비어 있는지 확인한다.
3단계 : 고정 하부 몸통 핀을 열고 아래로 당긴다.
4단계 : 반동 스프링 제거.
5단계 : 볼트 캐리어와 충전 핸들 탈거.
6단계 : 볼트 캐리어에서 점화_핀 및 볼트 탈거.
7단계 : 분해 완료.

7.5.3 조립 과정 M4

조립 과정은 분해의 역과정이다.
1단계 : 노리쇠 캐리어에 볼트를 부착하고 핀을 끼운다.
2단계 : 장착 손잡이와 볼트 캐리어를 몸통에 부착한다.
3단계 : 하부 몸통에 반동 스프링을 부착한다.
4단계 : 하부 몸통을 닫고 핀을 누른다.
5단계 : 탄창 부착.
6단계 : 조립 완료.

8 기초통계연산의 예

부사관은 평균 · 합계 · 빈도 등 기본적인 통계기법을 활용해 근무상황에서 데이터의 특성과 동향을 파악해야 한다.

단위 주변에서 많은 통계를 볼 수 있다. 다양한 작업을 수행할 때 어떤 기준을 통계적인 방법을 사용할지 깊이 있게 고민할 필요가 있다.

- 과제의 결과를 발표하는 경우.
- 타 조직과의 효율성 비교할 경우.

8.1 통계란 무엇인가?

(참조:https://ncs.go.kr/th03/TH0302List.do?dirSeq=122)

통계는 어떤 현상의 상태를 양별로 반영하는 숫자이며, 특히 사회집단의 상황을 숫자로 표현한다.

최근에는 통계방법의 급속한 발전과 확산으로 자연현상이나 추상적 수치집단을 포함한 모든 집단현상을 통계라고 부른다. 따라서 통계는 불확실한 상황에서 현명한 결정을 내릴 수 있는 이론과 방법을 다루는 분야로 주로 자료 수집, 분류, 분석, 해석의 체계를 갖추고 있다.

통계 분석은 알려지지 않은 값을 알려진 값으로 바꾸는 과정이라고 할 수 있다.

통계 절차

통계 절차는 4단계로 이루어진다. 첫째, 대량의 데이터를 수정 가능하고 이해하기 쉬운 형태로 줄인다. 둘째, 표본을 통해 그룹의 특징을 추론한다. 셋째, 보조의사결정방법이 된다. 넷째, 논리적으로 특정한 결과를 추출하고 관찰 가능한 데이터를 통해 확인한다.

8.2 평균, 빈도 및 백분율

범위

관측치의 산란 정도를 나타내는 도구로서 최대값과 최소값으로 파악한 범위로, 최대값에서 최소값을 뺀 후 1을 더하는 것을 의미한다.

예를 들어, A가 2,3, 4, 5, 6, 7 포인트를 획득하는 경우 최대값은 7이고 최소값은 3이므로 A의 범위는 7-2+1=6이다.

평균

평균에는 모든 관측치에 대한 정보가 포함되어 있으므로 목표 그룹의 특성이 내포될 수 있는 값이다. 평균에는 산술 평균과 가중 평균이 있다.

산술평균

산술평균은 모든 관측치를 더하고 관측치의 수로 나누어 얻은 값을 말한다.

A의 그룹 =(2+3+4+5+6+7)/5 = 5.4의 평균

가중평균

가중 평균은 각 관측치에 데이터의 상대 가중치를 곱하고 부가가치를 가중치의 합으로 나누어 계산한다.

빈도수

빈도란 사건이 발생하거나 증상이 나타나는 정도를 말하며 빈도분포는 그러한 빈도를 표나 그래프에 포괄적이고 명확하게 표시하는 것을 말한다. 주파수 분포는 주파수와 백분율로 표현되며 상대 주파수 분포와 누적 주파수 분포로 나뉜다.

백분율

백분율은 100의 총 수량으로, 그 중 표현할 수량이 얼마나 되는지 나타낸다. 기호는 %이고 1/100은 1%이다. 백분율은 원형 그래프를 사용하면 쉽게 이해할 수 있다.

분산

분산은 특정 구체적인 수치로 데이터의 확산 정도를 나타내는 도구이다. 각 관측값과 평균값 사이의 간극을 제곱하여 더하고, 그 값을 총 **횟수로 나눈다**.

예제 : 3, 5, 7, 9의 분산

평균 = 3+5+7+9 = 24 ÷ 4 = 8

분산 = (3-8)2+(5-8)2+(7-8)2+(7-8)2+(7-8)2 ÷ 4 = 9

표준 편차

편차는 분산의 제곱근 값이다. 표준 편차는 평균으로부터 얼마나 떨어져 있는지를 나타내는 개념이다.

예제: 3, 5, 7, 9의 분산

평균 = 3+5+7+9 = 24 ÷ 4 = 8

분산 = (3-8)2+(5-8)2+(7-8)2+(9-8)2+(9-8)2 ÷ 4 = 9

표준 편차 = 3

표준편차가 크면 데이터가 넓게 퍼져 이질성이 크다는 뜻이고, 작으면 데이터가 집중돼 동질성이 커진다.

8.3 5개 숫자 요약

평균과 표준편차만으로는 원본 데이터의 전체적인 형태를 파악하기가 어렵다. 따라서 최소값, 최대값, 중간값, 하위 25% 값, 상위 25% 값을 사용하는 것을 다섯 가지 숫자 요약이라고 한다.

최소값은 원본 데이터 중 값이 가장 작은 값을 의미하고, 최대값은 데이터 중 값이 가장 큰 값을 의미한다.

중간값은 정확히 가운데에 위치한 값을 의미한다. 하위 25% 값과 상위 25% 값은 원본 데이터를 크기 순서대로 정렬하여 4등분한다. 이 값을 사용하여 위쪽과 아래쪽 레이어 사이의 경계를 식별할 수 있다.

8.4 M240 총기명칭

8.4.1 M240 스펙

M240 기관총은 7.62 × 51 mm NATO 탄을 사용하는 미군의 탄띠급탄식 중기관총이다. FN MAG 기관총을 바탕으로 개발되었다. M240 기관총은 점차 미군에 주 기관총 이었던 M60 기관총을 대체하고 있다.

9 차트의 분석과 작성 능력

9.1 차트의 종류

막대 차트

막대 차트는 비교하고자 하는 수량을 막대의 길이로 표시하여 그 길이를 비교하고 각 수량간의 대소 관계를 나타내는 그래프이다. 자료의 내역 , 비교, 경과, 도수 등을 표시하는 용도로 활용하고자 할 때 막대 차트를 사용한다.

막대가 가로로 놓여 있을 경우에는 막대형 차트, 세로로 놓여 있을 경우에는 세로 막대형 차트라고 해서 구분하기도 한다.

선(절선)형 차트

선(절선) 차트는 시간의경과에 따른 수량의 변화를 절선의 기울기로 나타내는 차트로 경과, 비교분포를 비롯하여 상관관계를 나타내기 위해 사용한다.

이 차트의 가장 기본적인 활용은 연도별 자료의 변화와 같은 시간적 추이를 표시하는데 적합하다.

원형 차트

원 차트는 내역이나 내용의 구성비를 원을 분할하여 작성하는 차트이다. 전체 100%에 대한 구성비를 표현할 때 다양하게 활용할 수 있다.

방사형 차트

방사형 차트는 거미줄 차트라고도 하며 비교하는 수량을 직경 또는 반경으로 나누어 원의 중심에서의 거리에 따라 각 수량의 관계를 나타내는 그래프로서 각 요소를 비교하거나 경과를 나타낼 때 활용할 수 있다.

점 차트

점 차트는 가로축과 세로축에 2요소를 두고, 알고자 하는 것이 어떤 위치에 있는가를 알고자 할 때 작성하는 차트이다. 점 차트는 지역분포를 비롯하여 도시, 지방, 기업, 상품 등의 평가나 위치, 성격을 표시하는 용도로 활용한다.

9.2 차트 분석 능력

필요한 지식 수준

대부분의 경우 도표를 해석하는 데는 특별한 지식이 필요하지 않는다. 다만 지식의 수준에는 차이가 있기 때문에 상식은 어떤 이들에게는 지식일 수 있다. 따라서 부사관으로서 업무와 관련된 기초지식 습득을 통해 특수지식을 일반지식으로 일반화할 필요가 있다.

차트에 표시된 데이터의 의미를 정확하게 이해

주어진 차트의 자료를 실수로 해석하는 경우 데이터의 실제 의미를 확장하여 해석할 수 있다. 예를 들어 부사관 보병대 지원자가 많다고 해서 해당 부서가 지원자를 대거 선발하는 것은 아니기 때문에 같은 것으로 착각할 수 있다.

차트에서 아는 것과 모르는 것의 구별

주어진 차트의 데이터로 부터 알려진 것과 알려지지 않은 것을 완전히 구별할 필요가 있다. 즉, 주어진 도표에서 의미를 확장하고 해석하는 것은 곤란하고, 주어진 도표를 바탕으로 자신의 주장을 충분히 추론할 수 있는 보편적인 타당한 근거가 제시되어야 한다.

총액 증가와 비율 증가의 차이

같은 비율이라도 총량에는 많은 차이가 있을 수 있다. 또한 비율의 차이가 있더라도 총양을 표시하지 않으면 비율의 차이를 기준으로 절대 양을 평가할 수 없으므로 신중한 검토가 요구된다.

백분위수와 사분위수의 이해

백분위수는 크기순으로 배열한 자료를 100등분 하는 수의 값을 의미한다. 예를 들어 제90 백분위수란 자료를 크기순으로 나열했을 때 90%의 관찰값이 그 값보다 작거나 같고, (100-90%)의 관찰값이 그 값보다 크거나 같게 되는 값을 말한다.

사분위란 자료를 4등분한 것으로 제1사분위수는 제25백분위수, 제2사분위수는 제50백분위수(중앙치), 제3사분위수는 제75백분위수에 해당되며 나머지는 백분위수에 해당되게 된다.

9.3 차트 작성 능력

다양한 문서 편집기에서 표 만들기와 차트 만들기 기능을 제공하고 있다. 차트를 만들기 위해선 먼저 표를 이용하여 자료를 제공하고 이를 목적에 맞는 차트로 만들어야 한다. 이번 절에서는 엑셀프로그램을 사용해서 차트 만드는 방법에 대해 알아본다.

9.3.1 막대 차트 만들기

막대 차트는 비교하고자 하는 수량을 막대의 길이로 표시하여 그 길이를 비교하고 각 수량간의 대소 관계를 나타내는 그래프이다. 다음 표를 만들고 막대형 차트로 만들어 보자.

① 메인 메뉴에서 테이블을 선택하고 다음 그림과 같이 5x4 데이터를 입력한다.
② 위의 표를 막대 차트로 변경하려면 삽입 → 권장 차트 → 막대 차트 메뉴를 선택한다.
③ 여러 유형의 막대 차트 중에서 첫 번째 차트인 2차원 막대 차트를 선택하면 다음 차트를 볼 수 있다.
④ 차트의 구성 요소는 축, 축 주제, 차트 제목, 데이터 레이블, 데이터 테이블, 오류 스틱, 눈금 선, 범례 및 추세선이다. 먼저 차트 주제를 변환하려면 제목을 두 번 클릭해 'Number of Soldier'를 변경한다.
⑤ 범례를 변경하려면 범례를 선택하고 마우스 오른쪽 버튼을 눌러 데이터를 클릭한다.
⑥ 화면에서 첫 번째 범례 및 수평 축 레이블 항목을 해제한다. 범례 항목을 "단위"로 변경하려면 편집 버튼을 누른다. 다음 그림과 같이 범례에 따른 각 유닛의 구성원 수가 올바르게 차트화 된다.
⑦ 다음 그림과 같이 상세 항목을 편집하려면 각 차트 요소를 선택하고 수정할 수 있다.
⑧ 다른 유형의 차트로 변경하려면 차트 변경 메뉴를 선택하여 변경된 차트를 반영한다.

9.3.2 선 차트 만들기

꺾은선형 차트는 시간 경과에 따른 수량 변화를 점선의 기울기로 나타내는 차트로 진행률, 비교분포 등 상관관계를 나타내는 데 사용된다. 부대별 병사 수가 연도별로 달라지는 것은 쉽게 이해할 수 있다.

위의 예에서 막대 차트를 선형 차트로 변경하면 각 연도별 병력 수의 변화 정도를 쉽게 파악할 수 있습니다.

Question Answer [문제 해답]

1.Q 질문

1. 부사관의 장점은 무엇이라 생각합니까?

평생직장 보장, 최단 기간에 목돈 마련, 복지 혜택으로 실질 임금 상승, 연금혜택을 통한 정년 보장, 자기 개발의 기회제공, 폭 넓은 자녀교육 지원

2. 다음 4가지 중 속성이 다른 것은 무엇입니까?

① 상사   ② 대위   ③ 중사   ④ 일등상사

정 답 : ② 대위

3. 부사관의 목표는 무엇입니까?

부사관은 스스로 빛남으로서 명예를 추구하고 자부심을 갖는다. 부사관은 사회적 인간으로서 지켜야할 원칙을 지각하고 행동할 수 있어야 한다. 그들은 모든 일들에 있어 올바른 사고와 판단으로 건설적인 제안과 개인보다는 다른 사람을 먼저 살피는 방법을 아는 사회 공동체 의식을 견지할 수 있어야 한다.

4. 다음 문장을 한국어로 번역하세요.

4-1. 대한민국 육군은 국방의 중심입니다.

4-2. 군의 존재 목적은 궁극적으로 전쟁에서 승리하고 국가를 보존하는 것입니다.

4-3. ROKA는 전쟁 발생을 막는데 기여합니다.

4-4. 체계화된 통신 지휘 제어에 의한 전투력 관리를 위한 동시 통합 보장.

4-5. 부사관은 직무에 능통하고, 모든 일에 솔선수범하며, 병사의 법질서 준수를 감독한다.

5. Translate the following sentence into English.

5-1. Noncommissioned officers play a bridge role between officers and soldiers in the military.

5-2. Noncommissioned officers perform duties as experts in equipment management, weapon maintenance, and unit management within the military.

5-3. The well-being and future of the Republic of Korea depend on the ROK Armed Forces.

2.Q **질문**

1. ROKA의 3가지 역할은 무엇입니까?

① 보장자 : 전쟁억제, 작전적 신속대응, 결전바위, 안전 보장

② 구축자 : 남북 신뢰형상 및 평화구축 지원, 국민의 안전지원 국제 평화유지 및 군사외교

③ 연결자 :의무복무의 가치제고 사회 경쟁력을 겸비한 간부육성 과학기술 산업 경제발전 기여

2. 다음 중 육군의 3대 목표가 아닌 것은 어느 것인가?

① 전쟁 억지력   ② 인재 양성   ③ 적을 공격   ④ 국민에게 봉사

정답 ③

3. 육군 참조총장의 의무는 무엇입니까?

국방장관의 명령에 따라 육군 헌병대의 지휘 · 감독을 하되, 전투를 주된 임무로 하는 각 복무의 작전부대에 대한 지휘 · 감독은 제외한다.

4. 다음 문장을 한국어로 번역하세요.

4-1. 다른 부대들은 특수전, 항공작전, 지속전략 지원, 교육훈련, 예비군 엘리트주의, 행정지원 등을 수행한다.

4-2. 권총이란 위 또는 양손으로 취급할 수 있는 개인용 소화기를 말합니다.

4-3. ROKA의 존재 목적은 궁극적으로 전쟁에서 승리하고 국가를 보존하는 것이지만 싸우지 않고 승리하는 것이 최선입니다.

4-4. 전투원 안전대책도 철저히 준비하였습니다.

4-5. 육군이 초급 부사관으로 구성된 전투단을 편성해 KCTC 훈련을 한 것은 이번이 처음이다.

5. Translate the following sentence into English.

5-1. The Republic of Korea Army contributes to the suppression of war as a central force of national defense.

5-2. The Army Chief of Staff directs and supervises the Army according to the order of the President.

5-3. The purpose of the military's existence is to preserve the state by winning the war.

4.Q 질문

1. 군인의 개개인 공통 기본 훈련은 무엇입니까?

병사 개개인이 전장에서 싸우고, 살아남고, 승리하기 위한 14개의 필수 훈련이다.
정보를 획득하여 14개 기본 필수훈련에 대해 설명하시오.

2. 다음 예에서 네 가지 속성 중 잘못된 분류는 무엇입니까?

① 을지포커스 훈련　　② 수도 수복 훈련　　③ 연대전투단 훈련　　④ 독수훈련
정답 :②

3. 응급처치 4단계를 설명하시오.

첫 번째, 기도유지
둘째, 출혈을 멈추게 하며
셋째, 충격을 예방하고 치료를 계속한다.
마지막으로, 상처를 보호한다.

4. 다음 문장을 한국어로 번역하세요.

4-1. 주간이동 훈련의 목적은 군인들이 적의 감시와 포격 아래 목표물에 신속하게 접근할 수 있
도록 하는 것이다.

4-2. 정보수집 교육은 다음과 같은 방식으로 진행됩니다.

4-3. 병사 개개인의 공통 훈련은 병사 개개인이 전장에서 싸우고, 살아남고, 승리하기 위한 필수
훈련이다.

4-4. 을지 포커스 렌즈 훈련의 목적은 전반적인 전투태세와 동원 태세를 포함한 필요한 조치를 점검하는 것이다.

4-5. 독수리 훈련 전시에 한미연합작전 당시 후방지역의 전투지원 및 전투 복무지원 시설을 보호하는 것이 목적이다.

5. Write down the following sentence into English.

5-1. Controllers and umpires throughly prepare it by war game.

5-2. The period of training cycle is a period from the start of the individual training to the end of battalion tactical training.

5-3. The basic principle of shotgun is to attack the face rather than the point in selecting the target.

5.Q Qustion

Write the meaning of abbreviation.

Abbreviation	meaning
AA	Air to Air 공대공, Asembly Area 집결지, Anti-Aircraft 대공
AAM	Air to Air Missile 공대공 미사일
ABC	Atomic, Biological, Chemical 화생방
AAM	Air to Air Missile 공대공 미사일
AFKN	American Forces Korea Network 한국내 미국방송
AMMO	Ammunition 실탄
AP	Ammunition Point 탄약 분배소, Armor Piercing 철갑탄, Auto Pilot
ASM	Air to Surface Missile 공대지 유도 미사일
BM	Ballistic Missile
BP	Battle Position 전투진지
C4	Command, Control and Communications and Computer
CCT	Combat Control Team 전투 통제반
COP	Command Observation Post 지휘 관측소
DMZ	DeMilitarized Zone 비무장지대
GIS	Geographic Inforamtion System 지리정보체계
GOP	Ground Obsercation Post 지상관측소
ICBM	InterContinental Ballistic Missile 대륙간 탄도 미사일
IRBM	Intermediate Range Ballistic Missile 중거리탄도 미사일
JSA	Joint Security Area 공동경비구역
KADIZ	Korea Air Defence Identification Zone 한국방공식별구역
LRBM	Long Range Ballistic Missile 장거리 탄도 미사일
MRBM	Middle Range Ballistic Missile
NATO	North Atlantic Treaty Organization 북대서양 조약기
SRBM	Short Range Ballistic Missile 단거리 탄도 유도탄
THAAD	Terminal High Altitud Area Defence
WATCHCON	Watch Condition 대북정보감시태세

6.Q 질문

1. 수학 능력이 어떻게 되나요?

2. 다음 예에서 네 가지 속성 중 잘못된 분류는 무엇입니까?

① 더하기   ② 나누기   ③ 곱하기   ④ 지수

정답 : ④

3. 데이터 해석에 필요한 4가지 능력은 무엇입니까?

기초연산능력, 기초 통계능력, 기초 도표이해 능력, 기초 도표작성 능력

4. 다음 문장을 한국어로 번역하세요.

4-1. 조립 과정은 분해의 역과정입니다.

4-2. 주파수, 평균, 범위 계산을 통한 데이터 표현.

4-3. 기본 전산능력, 기초통계능력, 차트분석능력, 차트작성능력 등 4가지 하위역량이 있다.

4-4. 정상수준의 임원들은 업무 상황에 따라 2~3개의 차트를 사용하여 내용을 비교하고 발표한다.

4-5. 데이터 해석은 4가지 하위 역량을 가진 수학적 능력입니다.

5. Write down the following sentence into English.

5-1. In order to become a noncommissioned officer, you must pass the first written examination for military officers.

5-2. Repair ability requires an understanding of knowledge, skills, and work conditions.

5-3. Magnum belongs to a class of pistols.

7.Q 질문

1. 9거법은 무엇인가?

해설 : 4칙연산에서 각자리의 수를 9로 만들어 쉽게 계산하기 위해 인도에서 개발된 계산법

2. 빵 세 개를 다섯 명에게 어떻게 나누어 주나요?

해설: 먼저 빵 두 개를 반씩 나누어 4명에게 각각 1/2씩을 주고 나머지 빵 1개를 1/2로 나누어 나
머지 한명에게 1/2을 주고 나머지 1/2은 1/5로 나누면 된다.

3. 다음 사진에서 직사각형이 될 확률은 얼마입니까?

정답 : 4/5

해설 :정사각형의 개수 1(큰거)+4(작은거) 직사각형의 개수 가로 세로 4개

4. 다음 문장을 한국어로 번역하세요.

4-1. 9거법을 사용하면 나머지를 계산하기가 쉬워집니다.

4-2. 덧셈과 곱셈은 교환법, 연상법, 유통법을 포함한다.

4-3. 처음부터 세 개의 빵을 네 조각으로 나누는 것은 어렵습니다.

4-4. 고대 인도의 베다 수학은 현대 수학의 기원으로 인식되고 있습니다.

4-5. 분수는 분모와 지명자로 대표되는 나눗셈의 또 다른 표현입니다.

5. Write down the following sentence into English.

5-1. The four fundamental arithmetic operations mean addition, subtraction, multiplication, and division.

5-2. Decomposition and assembly of firearms.

5-3. The check nine is a calculation method for convenient verification.

8.Q 질문

1. 다섯 숫자 요약이란 무엇인가?

해설 : 평균과 표준편차만으로는 원본 데이터의 전체적인 형태를 파악하기가 어렵다. 따라서 최소값, 최대값, 중간값, 하위 25% 값, 상위 25% 값을 사용하는 것을 다섯 가지 숫자 요약이라고 한다.

2. 분산과 표준 편차의 의미는 무엇인가?

해설:

분산: 특정 구체적인 수치로 데이터의 확산 정도를 나타내는 도구이다. 각 관측값과 평균값 사이의 간극을 제곱하여 더하고, 그 값을 총 횟수로 나눈다.

표준 편차: 분산의 제곱근 값이다. 표준 편차는 평균으로부터 얼마나 떨어져 있는지를 나타내는 개념이다.

3. 통계과정을 설명하시오.

해설 : 통계 절차는 4단계로 이루어진다. 첫째, 대량의 데이터를 수정 가능하고 이해하기 쉬운 형태로 줄인다. 둘째, 표본을 통해 그룹의 특징을 추론한다. 셋째, 보조의사결정방법이 된다. 넷째, 논리적으로 특정한 결과를 추출하고 관찰 가능한 데이터를 통해 확인한다.

4. 다음 문장을 한국어로 번역하세요.

4-1. 통계는 어떤 현상의 상태를 양별로 반영하는 숫자이며, 특히 사회집단의 상황을 숫자로 표현한다.

4-2. 평균에는 모든 관측치에 대한 정보가 포함되어 있으므로 목표 그룹의 특성이 내포될 수 있는 값이다.

4-3. 빈도란 사건이 발생하거나 증상이 나타나는 정도를 말하며 빈도분포는 그러한 빈도를 표나 그래프에 포괄적이고 명확하게 표시하는 것을 말한다.

4-4. 표준편차가 크면 데이터가 넓게 퍼져 이질성이 크다는 뜻이고, 작으면 데이터가 집중돼 동질성이 커진다.

4-5. 최소값은 원본 데이터 중 값이 가장 작은 값을 의미하고, 최대값은 데이터 중 값이 가장 큰 값을 의미한다.

5. Write down the following sentence into English.

5-1. 중간값은 정확히 가운데에 위치한 값을 의미한다. 하위 25% 값과 상위 25% 값은 원본 데이터를 크기 순서대로 정렬하여 4등분한다.

5-2. D표준편차가 크면 데이터가 넓게 퍼져 이질성이 크다는 뜻이고, 작으면 데이터가 집중돼 동질성이 커진다.

5-3. 표준 편차는 평균으로부터 얼마나 떨어져 있는지를 나타내는 개념이다.

9.Q 질문

1. 막대형 그래프

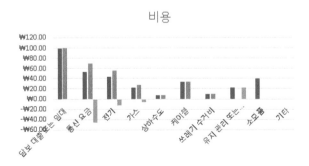

2. 방사형 차트

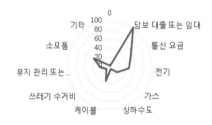

3. 원형 그래프

Author's Profile

박경배 (gbpark@yit.ac.kr)
- 명지대학교 전자공학과 학사
- 명지대학교 전자공학과 석사
- 명지대학교 전자공학과 박사
- 현대전자 멀티미디어 연구소 역임
- 여주대학교 소프트웨어융합과 교수
- 현) 여주대학교 국방장비과 교수
- 관심분야 가상현실, 국방 전산, 국방 무기

<출판저서>
2012 가상현실 증강현실과 VRML
2020 가상현실을 위한 HTML5 & Web3D
2021 HTML5 중심의 CSS3 & javascript

김지한 (kjh2135@naver.com)
- 성균관대학교 체육교육학 학사
- 성균관대학교 교육학 석사
- 청주대학교 국방안보학 박사
- 학군 25기(ROTC) 임관 및 육군 소령 예편
- 현) 여주대학교 군사학부 국방장비과 학과장
- 관심분야 : 군 특성화고, 국방안보, 국방체육, 리더십

군간부를 위한 군사영어

1판 1쇄 인쇄 2022년 02월 24일
1판 1쇄 발행 2022년 03월 02일
저   자 박경배·김지한
발 행 인 이범만
발 행 처 **21세기사** (제406-00015호)
경기도 파주시 산남로 72-16 (10882)
Tel. 031-942-7861   Fax. 031-942-7864
E-mail : 21cbook@naver.com
Home-page : www.21cbook.co.kr
ISBN 979-11-6833-015-3

정가 23,000원